50 Kid Breakfast Recipes for Home

By: Kelly Johnson

Table of Contents

- Pancake Puffs
- Mini Waffles
- Fruit and Yogurt Parfait
- Breakfast Quesadilla
- Smoothie Bowl
- Egg Muffins
- Oatmeal with Toppings
- Banana Pancakes
- French Toast Sticks
- Cheesy Breakfast Burrito
- Cinnamon Roll Casserole
- Apple Cinnamon Oatmeal
- Berry Smoothie Popsicles
- Mini Frittatas
- Breakfast Pizza
- Nut Butter and Banana Toast
- Yogurt and Fruit Smoothie
- Breakfast Sandwich
- Apple Cheddar Scones
- Egg and Veggie Wrap
- Coconut Chia Pudding
- Whole Wheat Banana Muffins
- Avocado Toast with Egg
- Cheese and Ham Croissants
- Breakfast Burrito Bowl
- Healthy Breakfast Cookies
- Granola and Fruit Parfait
- Scrambled Egg Tacos
- Peach Oat Bars
- Homemade Breakfast Sausage Patties
- Berry Muffins
- Spinach and Feta Egg Bites

- Cream Cheese and Jelly Bagels
- Mini Pancake Skewers
- Breakfast Smoothie
- Pumpkin Spice Oatmeal
- Almond Butter Apple Sandwiches
- Breakfast Tostadas
- Fruit Salad with Honey Lime Dressing
- Cheesy Spinach Stuffed Biscuits
- Sweet Potato Hash Browns
- Baked Eggs in Avocado
- Whole Wheat Waffles
- Breakfast Quesadilla Roll-Ups
- Berry Chia Jam Toast
- Oatmeal Breakfast Bars
- Zucchini Bread Muffins
- Breakfast Fruit Kabobs
- Cinnamon Apple Overnight Oats
- Egg and Cheese Breakfast Wrap

Pancake Puffs

Ingredients:

- 1 cup all-purpose flour
- 2 tablespoons sugar
- 1 tablespoon baking powder
- 1/2 teaspoon salt
- 1 cup milk
- 1 large egg
- 2 tablespoons melted butter or oil
- 1 teaspoon vanilla extract
- Optional: chocolate chips, berries, or other mix-ins

Instructions:

1. **Preheat Oven:** Preheat your oven to 375°F (190°C). Grease a mini muffin tin or line it with paper liners.
2. **Mix Dry Ingredients:** In a large bowl, whisk together the flour, sugar, baking powder, and salt.
3. **Combine Wet Ingredients:** In another bowl, mix the milk, egg, melted butter (or oil), and vanilla extract.
4. **Combine:** Pour the wet ingredients into the dry ingredients and stir until just combined. Be careful not to overmix. Fold in any optional mix-ins if using.
5. **Fill Muffin Tin:** Spoon the batter into the mini muffin tin, filling each cup about 2/3 full.
6. **Bake:** Bake for 10-12 minutes, or until a toothpick inserted into the center comes out clean and the puffs are golden brown.
7. **Cool and Serve:** Allow the pancake puffs to cool slightly before serving. They're great on their own or with a dusting of powdered sugar, syrup, or fresh fruit.

Enjoy your Pancake Puffs! They make a fun and bite-sized breakfast option for kids.

Mini Waffles

Ingredients:

- 1 1/2 cups all-purpose flour
- 2 tablespoons sugar
- 1 tablespoon baking powder
- 1/2 teaspoon salt
- 1 cup milk
- 1/3 cup vegetable oil or melted butter
- 1 large egg
- 1 teaspoon vanilla extract

Instructions:

1. **Preheat Waffle Iron:** Preheat your mini waffle iron according to the manufacturer's instructions. If it needs to be greased, lightly brush with oil or use a non-stick spray.
2. **Mix Dry Ingredients:** In a large bowl, whisk together the flour, sugar, baking powder, and salt.
3. **Combine Wet Ingredients:** In another bowl, mix the milk, vegetable oil (or melted butter), egg, and vanilla extract.
4. **Combine:** Pour the wet ingredients into the dry ingredients and stir until just combined. The batter will be slightly lumpy; don't overmix.
5. **Cook Waffles:** Pour a small amount of batter onto the preheated mini waffle iron, spreading it slightly. Close the lid and cook according to the waffle iron's instructions, usually for about 2-3 minutes, or until the waffles are golden brown and crisp.
6. **Serve:** Carefully remove the mini waffles and repeat with the remaining batter. Serve warm with toppings like fresh fruit, syrup, or a dusting of powdered sugar.

Enjoy your mini waffles! They're perfect for a fun breakfast or even as a snack.

Fruit and Yogurt Parfait

Ingredients:

- 2 cups plain or vanilla Greek yogurt
- 2 tablespoons honey or maple syrup (optional, for sweetness)
- 1 cup granola
- 1 cup fresh mixed berries (such as strawberries, blueberries, raspberries)
- 1 banana, sliced (optional)
- 1 tablespoon chia seeds or flaxseeds (optional)

Instructions:

1. **Sweeten Yogurt (if desired):** If you like your yogurt a bit sweeter, mix the honey or maple syrup into the yogurt until well combined.
2. **Layer Parfait:** In individual serving glasses or bowls, start by adding a layer of yogurt at the bottom.
3. **Add Fruit:** Top the yogurt layer with a layer of fresh berries. You can also add banana slices or other fruits you like.
4. **Add Granola:** Sprinkle a layer of granola over the fruit.
5. **Repeat Layers:** Repeat the layers with the remaining yogurt, fruit, and granola until the glasses or bowls are filled.
6. **Top and Serve:** Finish with a dollop of yogurt, a few more pieces of fruit, and a sprinkle of granola on top. Add chia seeds or flaxseeds if using.
7. **Chill (optional):** You can serve the parfaits immediately or chill them in the refrigerator for about 30 minutes for a cooler treat.

Enjoy your Fruit and Yogurt Parfait! It's a great way to start the day with a healthy and tasty breakfast.

Breakfast Quesadilla

Ingredients:

- 2 large flour tortillas
- 1 cup shredded cheddar cheese (or any cheese of your choice)
- 2 large eggs
- 1/4 cup milk
- 1/2 cup cooked and crumbled breakfast sausage or bacon (optional)
- 1/4 cup finely chopped bell peppers or onions (optional)
- 1 tablespoon butter or oil, for cooking
- Salt and pepper, to taste

Instructions:

1. **Prepare Filling:** In a bowl, whisk together the eggs and milk. Season with a pinch of salt and pepper. If using, mix in the cooked sausage or bacon and any vegetables.
2. **Cook Eggs:** Heat a non-stick skillet over medium heat and add a small amount of butter or oil. Pour in the egg mixture and cook, stirring occasionally, until the eggs are fully cooked and scrambled. Remove from the skillet and set aside.
3. **Assemble Quesadilla:** Place one tortilla on a clean surface. Spread half of the shredded cheese evenly over the tortilla. Top with the scrambled eggs mixture, and then sprinkle the remaining cheese over the eggs. Place the second tortilla on top.
4. **Cook Quesadilla:** Wipe out the skillet and return it to medium heat. Add a small amount of butter or oil. Carefully place the assembled quesadilla in the skillet and cook for 2-3 minutes, or until the bottom is golden brown and the cheese starts to melt. Flip the quesadilla and cook the other side for an additional 2-3 minutes.
5. **Cut and Serve:** Remove from the skillet and let it cool slightly before cutting into wedges. Serve warm with salsa, sour cream, or avocado if desired.

Enjoy your Breakfast Quesadilla! It's a delicious and versatile breakfast option that kids will love.

Smoothie Bowl

Ingredients:

- **For the Smoothie Base:**
    - 1 cup frozen fruit (such as berries, mango, or bananas)
    - 1/2 cup Greek yogurt (plain or vanilla)
    - 1/2 cup milk (dairy or non-dairy)
    - 1 tablespoon honey or maple syrup (optional, for added sweetness)
    - 1/2 teaspoon vanilla extract (optional)
- **For Toppings:**
    - Fresh fruit (sliced strawberries, bananas, blueberries, etc.)
    - Granola
    - Nuts or seeds (such as chia seeds, flaxseeds, or almonds)
    - Shredded coconut
    - A drizzle of honey or nut butter

Instructions:

1. **Blend Smoothie Base:** In a blender, combine the frozen fruit, Greek yogurt, milk, honey (if using), and vanilla extract (if using). Blend until smooth and creamy. If the mixture is too thick, add a little more milk to reach your desired consistency.
2. **Pour into Bowl:** Pour the smoothie into a bowl.
3. **Add Toppings:** Arrange your desired toppings on the surface of the smoothie. You can get creative with patterns or just scatter them evenly.
4. **Serve Immediately:** Enjoy your smoothie bowl right away for the best texture and flavor.

Feel free to customize your smoothie bowl with any of your favorite fruits, nuts, or seeds. It's a great way to start the day with a healthy and satisfying breakfast!

Egg Muffins

Ingredients:

- 6 large eggs
- 1/4 cup milk (dairy or non-dairy)
- 1 cup shredded cheese (cheddar, mozzarella, or your choice)
- 1/2 cup diced cooked ham, bacon, or sausage (optional)
- 1/2 cup chopped vegetables (such as bell peppers, spinach, onions, or tomatoes)
- Salt and pepper, to taste
- Cooking spray or oil for greasing

Instructions:

1. **Preheat Oven:** Preheat your oven to 375°F (190°C). Grease a 12-cup muffin tin with cooking spray or lightly brush with oil.
2. **Prepare Egg Mixture:** In a large bowl, whisk together the eggs and milk. Season with salt and pepper to taste.
3. **Add Fillings:** Stir in the shredded cheese, diced meat (if using), and chopped vegetables.
4. **Fill Muffin Tin:** Pour the egg mixture evenly into the muffin tin cups, filling each about 3/4 full.
5. **Bake:** Bake in the preheated oven for 15-20 minutes, or until the egg muffins are set and lightly golden on top. A toothpick inserted into the center should come out clean.
6. **Cool and Serve:** Allow the egg muffins to cool slightly before removing them from the tin. They can be served warm or at room temperature.
7. **Storage:** Store any leftovers in an airtight container in the refrigerator for up to 5 days. Reheat in the microwave for about 30-60 seconds.

Feel free to customize these Egg Muffins with your favorite ingredients or whatever you have on hand. They're great for a quick breakfast and can be made ahead of time!

Oatmeal with Toppings

Ingredients:

- 1 cup old-fashioned rolled oats
- 2 cups milk (dairy or non-dairy) or water
- 1/4 teaspoon salt
- 1 tablespoon honey or maple syrup (optional, for sweetness)
- 1/2 teaspoon vanilla extract (optional)

Instructions:

1. **Cook Oats:** In a medium saucepan, bring the milk (or water) and salt to a boil. Add the oats and reduce the heat to low. Simmer, stirring occasionally, for about 5-7 minutes, or until the oats are soft and have absorbed most of the liquid.
2. **Sweeten and Flavor (optional):** Stir in honey or maple syrup and vanilla extract, if using. Adjust the sweetness to taste.
3. **Serve:** Spoon the oatmeal into bowls and add your choice of toppings.

Topping Ideas

1. **Fruit:**
    - Fresh berries (strawberries, blueberries, raspberries)
    - Sliced bananas
    - Diced apples or pears
    - Dried fruits (raisins, cranberries, apricots)
2. **Nuts and Seeds:**
    - Chopped nuts (almonds, walnuts, pecans)
    - Seeds (chia seeds, flaxseeds, sunflower seeds)
    - Nut butters (peanut butter, almond butter)
3. **Sweet Additions:**
    - A drizzle of honey or maple syrup
    - A sprinkle of brown sugar or cinnamon
    - A dollop of yogurt
4. **Crunchy Toppings:**
    - Granola
    - Shredded coconut
    - Cacao nibs or mini chocolate chips
5. **Savory Options:**
    - A sprinkle of shredded cheese
    - A few cooked bacon bits
    - A dash of salt and pepper

Additional Tips

- **Make Ahead:** Prepare a big batch of oatmeal and store it in the refrigerator for up to 5 days. Reheat individual portions in the microwave, adding a splash of milk if needed.
- **Overnight Oats:** For a no-cook option, mix oats with milk or yogurt and toppings, and let them soak in the refrigerator overnight.

Enjoy your oatmeal with your favorite toppings! It's a versatile and healthy breakfast that can be tailored to suit any taste.

Banana Pancakes

Ingredients:

- 1 ripe banana
- 2 large eggs
- 1/2 cup all-purpose flour
- 1/2 teaspoon baking powder
- 1/4 teaspoon salt
- 1/2 teaspoon vanilla extract (optional)
- 1/4 cup milk (dairy or non-dairy, optional, for thinning batter)
- Butter or oil, for cooking

Instructions:

1. **Prepare Banana:** In a medium bowl, mash the ripe banana with a fork until smooth.
2. **Add Eggs:** Crack the eggs into the bowl with the mashed banana and whisk until well combined.
3. **Mix Dry Ingredients:** In a separate bowl, mix together the flour, baking powder, and salt.
4. **Combine Mixtures:** Add the dry ingredients to the banana mixture and stir until just combined. If the batter seems too thick, add a bit of milk to reach your desired consistency. Stir in the vanilla extract if using.
5. **Preheat Pan:** Heat a non-stick skillet or griddle over medium heat. Lightly grease with butter or oil.
6. **Cook Pancakes:** Pour about 1/4 cup of batter onto the skillet for each pancake. Cook for 2-3 minutes, or until bubbles form on the surface and the edges start to look set. Flip and cook for another 1-2 minutes, or until golden brown and cooked through.
7. **Serve:** Serve the pancakes warm with your favorite toppings, such as fresh fruit, maple syrup, or a dusting of powdered sugar.

Tips

- **Banana Ripeness:** The riper the banana, the sweeter and more flavorful your pancakes will be.
- **Mix-ins:** Feel free to add chocolate chips, nuts, or berries to the batter for extra flavor.
- **Freezing:** You can freeze leftover pancakes in a single layer on a baking sheet, then transfer them to a zip-top bag for up to 2 months. Reheat in the toaster or microwave.

Enjoy your Banana Pancakes—perfect for a quick and tasty breakfast!

French Toast Sticks

Ingredients:

- 4 slices of bread (thick-cut or Texas toast works best)
- 2 large eggs
- 1/2 cup milk (dairy or non-dairy)
- 1 tablespoon sugar
- 1 teaspoon vanilla extract
- 1/2 teaspoon ground cinnamon
- Butter or oil, for cooking

Instructions:

1. **Prepare Bread:** Cut the slices of bread into sticks, about 1-inch wide.
2. **Mix Batter:** In a shallow dish, whisk together the eggs, milk, sugar, vanilla extract, and cinnamon until well combined.
3. **Coat Bread:** Dip each bread stick into the egg mixture, making sure to coat all sides. Allow any excess batter to drip off.
4. **Preheat Pan:** Heat a non-stick skillet or griddle over medium heat and lightly grease with butter or oil.
5. **Cook Sticks:** Place the coated bread sticks in the skillet and cook for 2-3 minutes on each side, or until golden brown and crispy.
6. **Serve:** Serve the French toast sticks warm with your favorite dipping sauces, such as maple syrup, honey, or fruit jam. You can also sprinkle them with powdered sugar or additional cinnamon if desired.

Tips

- **Bread Choice:** Day-old bread or slightly stale bread works well for French toast, as it soaks up the batter better without becoming too soggy.
- **Add-ins:** You can add a pinch of nutmeg to the batter or mix in a handful of chocolate chips for extra flavor.
- **Freezing:** To make a big batch, cook and cool the sticks, then freeze them in a single layer on a baking sheet. Transfer to a zip-top bag and reheat in the toaster or oven.

Enjoy your French Toast Sticks—they're a tasty and convenient breakfast option that kids will enjoy dipping and eating!

Cheesy Breakfast Burrito

Ingredients:

- 4 large flour tortillas
- 4 large eggs
- 1/4 cup milk (dairy or non-dairy)
- 1 cup shredded cheese (cheddar, Monterey Jack, or your choice)
- 1/2 cup cooked and crumbled breakfast sausage, bacon, or ham (optional)
- 1/2 cup diced bell peppers or onions (optional)
- 1 tablespoon butter or oil, for cooking
- Salt and pepper, to taste
- Salsa or hot sauce, for serving (optional)

Instructions:

1. **Prepare Filling:** In a bowl, whisk together the eggs, milk, salt, and pepper.
2. **Cook Eggs:** Heat a non-stick skillet over medium heat and add a small amount of butter or oil. Pour in the egg mixture and cook, stirring occasionally, until the eggs are scrambled and fully cooked. If using, add the cooked sausage, bacon, or ham, and vegetables during the last minute of cooking to warm them through.
3. **Assemble Burritos:** Warm the tortillas in the microwave or on a dry skillet until pliable. Place a portion of the scrambled egg mixture in the center of each tortilla. Sprinkle with shredded cheese.
4. **Fold Burritos:** Fold the sides of the tortilla over the filling, then roll up from the bottom to enclose the filling.
5. **Optional - Toast Burritos:** For a crispy exterior, wipe out the skillet and heat it over medium heat. Place the wrapped burritos seam-side down in the skillet and cook for 1-2 minutes on each side, or until golden brown and the cheese is melted.
6. **Serve:** Serve the burritos warm with salsa or hot sauce, if desired.

Tips

- **Make-Ahead:** Prepare and cook the burritos in advance. Wrap them individually in foil or plastic wrap and refrigerate for up to 3 days or freeze for up to 2 months. Reheat in the microwave or oven.
- **Customize:** Feel free to add other ingredients like avocado, black beans, or spinach to the filling.
- **Add Heat:** If you like a bit of spice, add diced jalapeños or hot sauce to the egg mixture.

Enjoy your Cheesy Breakfast Burrito—it's a tasty and customizable breakfast that's sure to please!

Cinnamon Roll Casserole

Ingredients:

- 2 cans (8 oz each) refrigerated cinnamon rolls with icing (or homemade cinnamon rolls, if preferred)
- 4 large eggs
- 1/2 cup milk (dairy or non-dairy)
- 1/4 cup maple syrup or honey
- 1 teaspoon vanilla extract
- 1/2 teaspoon ground cinnamon (optional, for extra cinnamon flavor)
- 1/4 cup chopped pecans or walnuts (optional, for added crunch)

Instructions:

1. **Preheat Oven:** Preheat your oven to 375°F (190°C). Grease a 9x13-inch baking dish or coat it with non-stick cooking spray.
2. **Prepare Cinnamon Rolls:** Open the cans of cinnamon rolls and separate each roll. Cut each roll into quarters. Place the quartered rolls in the prepared baking dish.
3. **Mix Custard:** In a large bowl, whisk together the eggs, milk, maple syrup (or honey), vanilla extract, and ground cinnamon (if using).
4. **Combine:** Pour the egg mixture evenly over the quartered cinnamon rolls in the baking dish. Gently stir to ensure the cinnamon rolls are coated with the custard mixture.
5. **Add Nuts (optional):** Sprinkle chopped pecans or walnuts over the top if using.
6. **Bake:** Bake in the preheated oven for 25-30 minutes, or until the casserole is set in the middle and the tops of the cinnamon rolls are golden brown.
7. **Add Icing:** While the casserole is baking, warm the icing that came with the cinnamon rolls in the microwave for about 10-15 seconds, or according to the package instructions.
8. **Serve:** Allow the casserole to cool for a few minutes before drizzling with the warmed icing. Serve warm.

Tips

- **Make-Ahead:** You can prepare the casserole the night before. Simply assemble the casserole and refrigerate overnight. In the morning, let it sit at room temperature for about 30 minutes before baking.
- **Add Fruit:** For extra flavor, consider adding fresh or frozen fruit, like berries or apples, into the casserole before baking.

Enjoy your Cinnamon Roll Casserole—it's a sweet and indulgent breakfast that's perfect for weekends or special occasions!

Apple Cinnamon Oatmeal

Ingredients:

- 1 cup old-fashioned rolled oats
- 2 cups milk (dairy or non-dairy) or water
- 1 large apple, peeled, cored, and diced
- 1/4 cup brown sugar or maple syrup (adjust to taste)
- 1 teaspoon ground cinnamon
- 1/4 teaspoon ground nutmeg (optional)
- 1/4 teaspoon salt
- 1 tablespoon butter or oil (optional, for extra richness)
- Optional toppings: chopped nuts, raisins, additional apple slices, a drizzle of honey, or a sprinkle of granola

Instructions:

1. **Cook Apples:** In a medium saucepan, melt the butter (if using) over medium heat. Add the diced apples and cook for 3-4 minutes, or until they start to soften. Stir occasionally.
2. **Add Spices and Sweetener:** Sprinkle the apples with ground cinnamon, nutmeg (if using), and brown sugar or maple syrup. Stir to coat the apples evenly. Cook for an additional 2-3 minutes, or until the apples are tender and the mixture is slightly caramelized.
3. **Prepare Oatmeal:** Add the oats and milk (or water) to the saucepan with the apples. Stir well and bring to a boil.
4. **Simmer:** Reduce the heat to low and simmer for 5-7 minutes, or until the oats are cooked and have absorbed most of the liquid. Stir occasionally to prevent sticking.
5. **Serve:** Spoon the oatmeal into bowls. Add any optional toppings you like, such as chopped nuts, raisins, extra apple slices, a drizzle of honey, or a sprinkle of granola.
6. **Enjoy:** Serve warm and enjoy a cozy, flavorful breakfast!

Tips

- **Make-Ahead:** You can prepare the apple mixture in advance and store it in the refrigerator for up to 3 days. Reheat and add to cooked oats when ready to serve.
- **Add-ins:** Customize your oatmeal with additional ingredients like chia seeds, flaxseeds, or protein powder for an extra boost.

This Apple Cinnamon Oatmeal is not only delicious but also packed with nutrients, making it a great way to start the day!

Berry Smoothie Popsicles

Ingredients:

- 1 cup fresh or frozen berries (such as strawberries, blueberries, raspberries, or a mix)
- 1 cup Greek yogurt (plain or vanilla)
- 1/2 cup milk (dairy or non-dairy) or fruit juice
- 2 tablespoons honey or maple syrup (adjust to taste)
- 1 teaspoon vanilla extract (optional)
- Optional: 1/2 banana for added creaminess

Instructions:

1. **Prepare Ingredients:** If using fresh berries, wash and hull them as needed. If using frozen berries, there's no need to thaw them.
2. **Blend:** In a blender, combine the berries, Greek yogurt, milk (or juice), honey or maple syrup, and vanilla extract. If you're using banana, add it to the blender. Blend until smooth.
3. **Taste and Adjust:** Taste the mixture and adjust the sweetness if needed by adding more honey or maple syrup. Blend again if you make any adjustments.
4. **Pour into Molds:** Pour the smoothie mixture into popsicle molds, leaving a small space at the top for expansion.
5. **Insert Sticks:** Insert popsicle sticks into the molds. If your molds don't have built-in sticks, you can use wooden sticks or plastic spoons.
6. **Freeze:** Place the molds in the freezer and freeze for at least 4-6 hours, or until completely frozen.
7. **Unmold and Serve:** To remove the popsicles, run the outside of the molds under warm water for a few seconds to loosen them. Gently pull the sticks to release the popsicles.
8. **Store:** Store any leftover popsicles in a zip-top bag or airtight container in the freezer for up to 2 weeks.

Tips

- **Variations:** You can mix and match different berries or add other fruits like mango, peaches, or kiwi to the blender for varied flavors.
- **Creamier Popsicles:** For a creamier texture, use full-fat Greek yogurt or add a bit of coconut milk.
- **Add-ins:** Consider adding a handful of spinach or kale for an extra boost of nutrition without altering the flavor too much.

Enjoy these Berry Smoothie Popsicles as a healthy snack or dessert—they're perfect for a hot day and easy to make!

Mini Frittatas

Ingredients:

- 6 large eggs
- 1/4 cup milk (dairy or non-dairy)
- 1/2 cup shredded cheese (cheddar, mozzarella, feta, or your choice)
- 1/2 cup cooked and crumbled bacon, sausage, or ham (optional)
- 1/2 cup chopped vegetables (such as bell peppers, spinach, onions, tomatoes, or mushrooms)
- 1 tablespoon olive oil or butter, for greasing
- Salt and pepper, to taste
- Optional: fresh herbs (such as parsley, chives, or thyme)

Instructions:

1. **Preheat Oven:** Preheat your oven to 375°F (190°C). Grease a 12-cup mini muffin tin or line it with paper liners.
2. **Prepare Ingredients:** If using vegetables, cook them in a skillet with a little olive oil or butter until tender. If using meat, cook and crumble it as needed.
3. **Mix Eggs:** In a large bowl, whisk together the eggs and milk. Season with salt and pepper.
4. **Combine Ingredients:** Stir in the shredded cheese, cooked meat (if using), and vegetables. Add fresh herbs if you're using them.
5. **Fill Muffin Tin:** Spoon the egg mixture evenly into the mini muffin tin cups, filling each about 2/3 full.
6. **Bake:** Bake in the preheated oven for 15-20 minutes, or until the frittatas are set in the center and lightly golden on top. A toothpick inserted into the center should come out clean.
7. **Cool and Serve:** Allow the mini frittatas to cool slightly before removing them from the tin. Serve warm or at room temperature.
8. **Storage:** Store any leftovers in an airtight container in the refrigerator for up to 5 days. Reheat in the microwave for about 30 seconds.

Tips

- **Make-Ahead:** Mini frittatas are great for meal prep. Make a batch and keep them in the fridge for a quick breakfast or snack.
- **Customization:** Feel free to customize the filling ingredients based on what you have on hand or your family's preferences.
- **Freezing:** You can freeze mini frittatas by placing them in a single layer on a baking sheet, then transferring them to a zip-top bag or airtight container. Reheat from frozen in the microwave or oven.

Enjoy your Mini Frittatas—perfect for a quick, nutritious meal that's easy to customize and enjoy!

Breakfast Pizza

Ingredients:

- **For the Crust:**
    - 1 pre-made pizza dough (store-bought or homemade) or a pre-baked pizza crust
    - 1 tablespoon olive oil (if using fresh dough)
- **For the Toppings:**
    - 1/2 cup pizza sauce or tomato sauce (optional)
    - 1 cup shredded cheese (cheddar, mozzarella, or your choice)
    - 4 large eggs
    - 1/2 cup cooked and crumbled bacon, sausage, or ham
    - 1/2 cup chopped vegetables (such as bell peppers, onions, spinach, mushrooms, or tomatoes)
    - Salt and pepper, to taste
    - Optional: fresh herbs (such as chives, parsley, or basil)

Instructions:

1. **Preheat Oven:** Preheat your oven to 425°F (220°C). If using fresh pizza dough, lightly grease a baking sheet or pizza stone with olive oil.
2. **Prepare Crust:** Roll out the pizza dough on a lightly floured surface to your desired thickness. Transfer it to the prepared baking sheet or pizza stone. If using a pre-baked crust, place it on the baking sheet.
3. **Pre-bake Dough (if needed):** If using fresh dough, pre-bake it for 5-7 minutes to set the crust before adding toppings.
4. **Add Sauce (optional):** Spread a thin layer of pizza sauce or tomato sauce over the crust, if desired.
5. **Add Cheese:** Sprinkle shredded cheese evenly over the crust.
6. **Add Toppings:** Distribute the cooked bacon, sausage, or ham over the cheese. Add the chopped vegetables.
7. **Add Eggs:** Crack the eggs and carefully place them on top of the pizza, spacing them out evenly. Season with a little salt and pepper.
8. **Bake:** Bake in the preheated oven for 12-15 minutes, or until the eggs are cooked to your desired level (whites should be set, and yolks should be slightly runny or fully cooked, depending on preference). The cheese should be melted and bubbly, and the crust should be golden brown.
9. **Garnish:** Remove the pizza from the oven and let it cool slightly. Garnish with fresh herbs if desired.
10. **Serve:** Slice and serve warm.

Tips

- **Customization:** Feel free to experiment with different toppings based on your family's preferences. Try adding avocado, sun-dried tomatoes, or different types of cheese.
- **Cooking Eggs:** If you prefer the eggs more cooked, you can cover the pizza with aluminum foil during the last few minutes of baking to ensure the eggs are fully set.

- **Vegetarian Option:** Skip the meat and add extra vegetables or a sprinkle of nutritional yeast for a vegetarian version.

Enjoy your Breakfast Pizza—it's a versatile and delicious way to start the day!

Nut Butter and Banana Toast

Ingredients:

- 2 slices of whole-grain or your favorite bread
- 2 tablespoons nut butter (peanut butter, almond butter, cashew butter, etc.)
- 1 ripe banana
- A drizzle of honey or maple syrup (optional)
- A sprinkle of cinnamon (optional)
- A pinch of sea salt (optional)
- Optional toppings: chia seeds, flaxseeds, granola, or chopped nuts

Instructions:

1. **Toast Bread:** Toast the slices of bread in a toaster or toaster oven until golden brown and crispy.
2. **Prepare Banana:** While the bread is toasting, peel the banana and slice it into thin rounds.
3. **Spread Nut Butter:** Once the toast is ready, spread an even layer of nut butter over each slice.
4. **Add Banana:** Arrange the banana slices on top of the nut butter.
5. **Optional Toppings:** Drizzle with a little honey or maple syrup if desired for extra sweetness. Sprinkle with cinnamon or a pinch of sea salt for added flavor. You can also add chia seeds, flaxseeds, granola, or chopped nuts for extra crunch and nutrition.
6. **Serve:** Enjoy immediately while the toast is still warm and the nut butter is slightly melted.

Tips

- **Nut Butter:** Use your favorite type of nut butter, or try mixing different kinds for variety.
- **Banana Ripeness:** For a sweeter taste, use a very ripe banana.
- **Add-ins:** Customize with additional fruit like berries or apple slices, or spread a layer of Greek yogurt before adding the banana for extra creaminess.
- **Storage:** This is best enjoyed fresh, but you can prepare the ingredients ahead of time and assemble just before eating.

Nut Butter and Banana Toast is a simple yet satisfying option that combines protein, healthy fats, and carbohydrates, making it a great choice for a quick breakfast or snack.

Yogurt and Fruit Smoothie

Ingredients:

- 1 cup Greek yogurt (plain or vanilla) or regular yogurt
- 1 cup fresh or frozen fruit (such as berries, bananas, mango, or peaches)
- 1/2 cup milk (dairy or non-dairy) or fruit juice
- 1-2 tablespoons honey or maple syrup (optional, for sweetness)
- 1/2 teaspoon vanilla extract (optional)
- 1/4 cup oats or chia seeds (optional, for added texture and nutrition)
- Ice cubes (optional, for a thicker smoothie)

Instructions:

1. **Prepare Ingredients:** If using fresh fruit, wash and cut it into chunks. If using frozen fruit, you can use it directly from the freezer.
2. **Blend:** In a blender, combine the yogurt, fruit, milk (or juice), honey or maple syrup (if using), and vanilla extract (if using). Add oats or chia seeds if desired.
3. **Blend Until Smooth:** Blend until the mixture is smooth and creamy. If the smoothie is too thick, you can add more milk or juice to reach your desired consistency. If using ice cubes, add them and blend until crushed and the smoothie is frothy.
4. **Taste and Adjust:** Taste the smoothie and adjust the sweetness if needed by adding more honey or maple syrup. Blend again if you make any adjustments.
5. **Serve:** Pour the smoothie into glasses and serve immediately.
6. **Optional Toppings:** You can top the smoothie with fresh fruit, granola, or a sprinkle of nuts or seeds for added texture and nutrition.

Tips

- **Fruit Combinations:** Experiment with different fruit combinations to find your favorite. For example, try a mix of strawberries, bananas, and blueberries for a berry smoothie, or mango and pineapple for a tropical twist.
- **Yogurt Choice:** Greek yogurt will make the smoothie thicker and creamier, while regular yogurt will be a bit lighter.
- **Sweetness:** Adjust the sweetness based on your fruit and personal preference. Some fruits are naturally sweeter than others.
- **Make-Ahead:** You can prepare smoothie packs by combining fruits and oats or chia seeds in freezer bags. When ready to make a smoothie, just add yogurt and milk or juice.

Enjoy your Yogurt and Fruit Smoothie—it's a versatile and healthy option that can be tailored to suit any taste!

Breakfast Sandwich

Ingredients:

- 2 slices of bread, English muffin halves, or a bagel (or your choice of sandwich bread)
- 1 large egg
- 1 slice of cheese (cheddar, Swiss, American, or your choice)
- 1-2 slices of cooked bacon, sausage patty, or ham (or a vegetarian alternative)
- 1-2 slices of tomato (optional)
- A few fresh spinach leaves or lettuce (optional)
- 1 tablespoon butter or oil, for cooking
- Salt and pepper, to taste
- Optional: avocado slices, hot sauce, or your favorite condiment

Instructions:

1. **Prepare Ingredients:** Cook the bacon, sausage, or ham if not using pre-cooked. Toast the bread, English muffin halves, or bagel in a toaster or toaster oven until lightly browned.
2. **Cook Egg:** Heat the butter or oil in a non-stick skillet over medium heat. Crack the egg into the skillet. Cook to your desired level of doneness—sunny-side up, over-easy, or scrambled. Season with salt and pepper.
3. **Assemble Sandwich:**
    - If using cheese, place a slice on one piece of the toasted bread or muffin.
    - Top with the cooked bacon, sausage, or ham.
    - Add the cooked egg on top of the meat.
    - Add tomato slices and spinach or lettuce if desired.
    - Spread avocado slices or add hot sauce or your favorite condiment if desired.
    - Top with the second piece of toast or muffin half.
4. **Serve:** Cut the sandwich in half if you like and serve immediately while warm.

Tips

- **Variations:** Feel free to customize your breakfast sandwich with different cheeses, meats, or vegetables. Try adding sautéed onions, peppers, or mushrooms for extra flavor.
- **Healthy Option:** Use whole-grain or multi-grain bread and add more veggies for a healthier twist.
- **Make-Ahead:** You can prepare components like cooked bacon, sausage patties, or scrambled eggs ahead of time and assemble the sandwiches in the morning.

Enjoy your Breakfast Sandwich—it's a hearty and delicious way to start your day!

Apple Cheddar Scones

Ingredients:

- 2 cups all-purpose flour
- 1/4 cup granulated sugar
- 1 tablespoon baking powder
- 1/2 teaspoon salt
- 1/2 cup (1 stick) cold unsalted butter, cut into small cubes
- 1 cup shredded sharp cheddar cheese
- 1 cup diced apple (peeled and cored, preferably a firm variety like Honeycrisp or Granny Smith)
- 1/2 cup milk (dairy or non-dairy)
- 1 large egg
- Optional: 1 tablespoon milk or cream for brushing
- Optional: Extra sugar for sprinkling on top

Instructions:

1. **Preheat Oven:** Preheat your oven to 400°F (200°C). Line a baking sheet with parchment paper or lightly grease it.
2. **Mix Dry Ingredients:** In a large bowl, whisk together the flour, sugar, baking powder, and salt.
3. **Cut in Butter:** Add the cold butter cubes to the flour mixture. Use a pastry cutter or your fingers to cut the butter into the flour until the mixture resembles coarse crumbs.
4. **Add Cheese and Apples:** Stir in the shredded cheddar cheese and diced apples.
5. **Prepare Wet Ingredients:** In a small bowl, whisk together the milk and egg.
6. **Combine:** Pour the milk mixture into the flour mixture. Stir until just combined. The dough will be slightly sticky.
7. **Shape Dough:** Turn the dough out onto a lightly floured surface and gently knead it a few times to bring it together. Pat it into a circle about 1 inch thick. Cut the dough into wedges or use a round cutter to cut out scones.
8. **Prepare for Baking:** Place the scones on the prepared baking sheet. If desired, brush the tops with a little milk or cream and sprinkle with extra sugar.
9. **Bake:** Bake for 15-18 minutes, or until the scones are golden brown and a toothpick inserted into the center comes out clean.
10. **Cool:** Allow the scones to cool slightly on a wire rack before serving.

Tips

- **Apple Choice:** Firm apples work best to prevent too much moisture from making the scones soggy.
- **Cheese:** Use a sharp cheddar for a more pronounced flavor.
- **Make-Ahead:** You can prepare the dough in advance and freeze it. Just cut the scones and freeze them on a baking sheet. Transfer them to a zip-top bag once frozen and bake from frozen, adding a few extra minutes to the baking time.

Enjoy your Apple Cheddar Scones—perfect with a cup of tea or coffee for a comforting treat!

Egg and Veggie Wrap

Ingredients:

- 1 large tortilla or wrap (whole wheat, flour, or your choice)

- 2 large eggs
- 1/4 cup milk (dairy or non-dairy)
- 1/2 cup shredded cheese (cheddar, mozzarella, or your choice)
- 1/2 cup diced vegetables (such as bell peppers, onions, spinach, tomatoes, mushrooms, or zucchini)
- 1 tablespoon olive oil or butter
- Salt and pepper, to taste
- Optional: hot sauce, salsa, or avocado for added flavor

Instructions:

1. **Prepare Vegetables:** Heat the olive oil or butter in a non-stick skillet over medium heat. Add the diced vegetables and cook for 3-5 minutes, or until tender. Season with a little salt and pepper. Transfer the vegetables to a plate and set aside.
2. **Cook Eggs:** In a bowl, whisk together the eggs and milk. Pour the mixture into the same skillet and cook over medium heat, stirring gently, until the eggs are scrambled and fully cooked. Stir in the shredded cheese until melted and combined.
3. **Assemble Wrap:**
   - Warm the tortilla in a dry skillet or microwave for a few seconds to make it more pliable.
   - Spread the cooked egg and cheese mixture evenly over the tortilla.
   - Top with the cooked vegetables.
4. **Wrap It Up:** Roll up the tortilla, folding in the sides as you go to create a neat wrap.
5. **Serve:** Slice in half if desired and serve warm.
6. **Optional Add-Ins:**
   - Add a spoonful of salsa or a drizzle of hot sauce for extra flavor.
   - Include slices of avocado or a sprinkle of fresh herbs like cilantro or chives.

Tips

- **Customization:** Feel free to use any vegetables you have on hand or adjust the cheese type based on your preference.
- **Protein Boost:** For extra protein, you can add cooked bacon, sausage, or ham.
- **Make-Ahead:** You can prepare the egg and veggie mixture in advance and store it in the refrigerator for up to 3 days. Reheat before assembling the wrap.
- **Vegetarian Option:** This recipe is already vegetarian-friendly. You can also add tofu or tempeh for added protein if you prefer.

Enjoy your Egg and Veggie Wrap—it's a versatile and tasty option that's easy to customize and perfect for a quick meal!

Coconut Chia Pudding

Ingredients:

- 1/2 cup chia seeds
- 1 can (13.5 oz) full-fat coconut milk (or coconut milk from a carton)
- 1/4 cup maple syrup or honey (adjust to taste)

- 1 teaspoon vanilla extract (optional)
- A pinch of salt

Optional Toppings:

- Fresh or dried fruit (e.g., berries, mango, banana, or pineapple)
- Nuts or seeds (e.g., almonds, coconut flakes, or chia seeds)
- Granola
- A drizzle of honey or maple syrup
- A sprinkle of cinnamon or nutmeg

Instructions:

1. **Mix Ingredients:** In a medium bowl, whisk together the chia seeds, coconut milk, maple syrup (or honey), vanilla extract (if using), and a pinch of salt until well combined.
2. **Refrigerate:** Cover the bowl and refrigerate for at least 4 hours or overnight. The chia seeds will absorb the liquid and expand, turning the mixture into a thick, pudding-like consistency. Stir the mixture halfway through the chilling time to ensure the chia seeds are evenly distributed and to prevent clumping.
3. **Serve:** Once the pudding has set, give it a good stir. Spoon it into individual serving dishes or bowls.
4. **Add Toppings:** Add your choice of toppings just before serving. Fresh fruit, nuts, seeds, granola, and a drizzle of honey or maple syrup all make great additions.
5. **Store:** Store any leftover chia pudding in an airtight container in the refrigerator for up to 5 days.

Tips

- **Sweetener:** Adjust the amount of sweetener based on your preference. You can also use other natural sweeteners like agave syrup or stevia.
- **Consistency:** If the pudding is too thick for your liking, you can stir in a bit more coconut milk to reach your desired consistency.
- **Flavor Variations:** Experiment with different flavors by adding cocoa powder, matcha powder, or a spoonful of fruit puree to the mixture before refrigerating.

Enjoy your Coconut Chia Pudding—it's a delicious and healthy treat that's easy to prepare and customize!

Whole Wheat Banana Muffins

Ingredients:

- 1 1/2 cups whole wheat flour
- 1/2 teaspoon baking soda
- 1/2 teaspoon baking powder

- 1/4 teaspoon salt
- 1/2 teaspoon ground cinnamon (optional)
- 1/2 cup coconut oil or unsalted butter, melted
- 1/2 cup honey or maple syrup
- 2 large ripe bananas, mashed (about 1 cup)
- 2 large eggs
- 1 teaspoon vanilla extract
- Optional: 1/2 cup chopped nuts (e.g., walnuts or pecans) or chocolate chips

Instructions:

1. **Preheat Oven:** Preheat your oven to 350°F (175°C). Line a 12-cup muffin tin with paper liners or lightly grease the cups.
2. **Mix Dry Ingredients:** In a medium bowl, whisk together the whole wheat flour, baking soda, baking powder, salt, and ground cinnamon (if using).
3. **Mix Wet Ingredients:** In a large bowl, combine the melted coconut oil or butter with the honey or maple syrup. Stir in the mashed bananas, eggs, and vanilla extract until well combined.
4. **Combine Mixtures:** Add the dry ingredients to the wet ingredients and mix until just combined. Be careful not to overmix. If using, fold in the chopped nuts or chocolate chips.
5. **Fill Muffin Cups:** Divide the batter evenly among the muffin cups, filling each about 2/3 full.
6. **Bake:** Bake in the preheated oven for 18-22 minutes, or until a toothpick inserted into the center of a muffin comes out clean.
7. **Cool:** Allow the muffins to cool in the tin for about 5 minutes, then transfer them to a wire rack to cool completely.

Tips

- **Bananas:** Use very ripe bananas for the best sweetness and flavor.
- **Sweetener:** Adjust the amount of honey or maple syrup based on your taste preferences. You can also use a combination of sweeteners.
- **Mix-Ins:** Customize your muffins by adding ingredients like dried fruit, seeds, or spices (e.g., nutmeg or cloves) to suit your preferences.
- **Storage:** Store muffins in an airtight container at room temperature for up to 3 days or freeze them for up to 3 months. To freeze, place muffins in a zip-top bag or airtight container and thaw at room temperature or microwave before serving.

Enjoy your Whole Wheat Banana Muffins—perfect for a healthy and satisfying snack or breakfast on the go!

Avocado Toast with Egg

Ingredients:

- 1 ripe avocado
- 2 slices of whole-grain or your favorite bread
- 2 large eggs
- 1 tablespoon olive oil or butter
- Salt and pepper, to taste

- Optional toppings: red pepper flakes, chopped fresh herbs (e.g., chives, cilantro, or parsley), a squeeze of lemon juice, or sliced cherry tomatoes

Instructions:

1. **Toast the Bread:** Toast the bread slices in a toaster or toaster oven until golden brown and crispy.
2. **Prepare the Avocado:** While the bread is toasting, cut the avocado in half, remove the pit, and scoop the flesh into a bowl. Mash the avocado with a fork until smooth, or leave it slightly chunky if you prefer. Season with salt and pepper to taste. You can also add a squeeze of lemon juice for extra flavor if desired.
3. **Cook the Eggs:**
   - **For Fried Eggs:** Heat olive oil or butter in a non-stick skillet over medium heat. Crack the eggs into the skillet and cook until the whites are set and the yolks are cooked to your liking (sunny-side up, over-easy, or medium). Season with salt and pepper.
   - **For Poached Eggs:** Bring a pot of water to a gentle simmer. Add a splash of vinegar (optional). Crack each egg into a small bowl, then gently slide it into the simmering water. Cook for 3-4 minutes, or until the whites are set but the yolk is still runny. Remove with a slotted spoon and drain on paper towels.
4. **Assemble the Toast:** Spread the mashed avocado evenly over the toasted bread slices.
5. **Top with Eggs:** Place the cooked eggs on top of the avocado toast. Season with additional salt and pepper if desired.
6. **Add Optional Toppings:** Sprinkle with red pepper flakes, fresh herbs, or any additional toppings you like. Add sliced cherry tomatoes or a drizzle of olive oil for extra flavor and nutrition.
7. **Serve:** Serve immediately while the toast is still warm and the eggs are fresh.

Tips

- **Avocado:** Choose ripe avocados that yield slightly when pressed. If your avocado is not ripe, you can speed up the ripening process by placing it in a paper bag with a banana for a day or two.
- **Egg Cooking:** Adjust the cooking time of the eggs based on your preference for yolk doneness. For runny yolks, aim for a shorter cooking time.
- **Variations:** Experiment with different toppings like smoked salmon, sautéed spinach, or feta cheese for added flavor and texture.

Enjoy your Avocado Toast with Egg—it's a satisfying and healthy meal that's quick to prepare and full of flavor!

Cheese and Ham Croissants

Ingredients:

- 1 sheet of puff pastry (store-bought or homemade)
- 4 ounces (about 1 cup) shredded cheese (e.g., cheddar, Swiss, or Gruyère)
- 4 slices of ham (deli ham or cooked ham, thinly sliced)
- 1 egg, beaten (for egg wash)
- Optional: a pinch of dried herbs (e.g., thyme, oregano) for extra flavor

Instructions:

1. **Preheat Oven:** Preheat your oven to 375°F (190°C). Line a baking sheet with parchment paper or a silicone baking mat.
2. **Prepare Puff Pastry:** Roll out the puff pastry sheet on a lightly floured surface. If using store-bought puff pastry, it usually comes in a pre-rolled sheet. Trim the edges to form a neat rectangle.
3. **Cut Pastry:** Cut the puff pastry into triangles or rectangles, depending on the size of the croissants you want to make. Typically, cutting the pastry into 4x4 inch squares and then cutting each square diagonally into triangles works well.
4. **Assemble Croissants:**
    - **For Triangles:** Place a slice of ham and a sprinkle of shredded cheese on the wide end of each triangle. Roll up from the wide end towards the point to form a croissant shape.
    - **For Rectangles:** Place a slice of ham and cheese on one half of each rectangle. Fold the other half over the filling to form a pocket or rectangle. Press the edges to seal.
5. **Brush with Egg Wash:** Place the assembled croissants on the prepared baking sheet. Brush the tops with the beaten egg to give them a golden, shiny finish.
6. **Add Herbs (Optional):** Sprinkle with dried herbs if desired for extra flavor.
7. **Bake:** Bake in the preheated oven for 15-20 minutes, or until the croissants are puffed up and golden brown.
8. **Cool:** Allow the croissants to cool slightly on a wire rack before serving.

Tips

- **Puff Pastry:** Use thawed puff pastry if it's frozen. Follow package instructions for thawing.
- **Cheese Options:** Experiment with different types of cheese or combine several types for a richer flavor.
- **Ham:** If using thick-cut ham, cut it into smaller pieces or strips to fit better inside the croissants.
- **Make-Ahead:** You can assemble the croissants in advance and freeze them before baking. Bake from frozen, adding a few extra minutes to the baking time.

Enjoy your Cheese and Ham Croissants—they're a delightful and savory treat that's sure to impress!

Breakfast Burrito Bowl

Ingredients:

- **For the Base:**
    - 1 cup cooked brown rice, quinoa, or your favorite grain (or use a base of hash browns or shredded potatoes)
- **For the Eggs:**
    - 4 large eggs
    - 1 tablespoon olive oil or butter
    - Salt and pepper, to taste
- **For the Toppings:**
    - 1/2 cup cooked black beans or pinto beans (drained and rinsed if using canned)
    - 1/2 cup diced tomatoes
    - 1/2 avocado, sliced or diced
    - 1/4 cup shredded cheese (cheddar, Monterey Jack, or your choice)
    - 1/4 cup salsa or pico de gallo
    - 1/4 cup chopped fresh cilantro (optional)
    - Lime wedges for serving
- **Optional Add-Ins:**
    - Sautéed bell peppers and onions
    - Sliced jalapeños or hot sauce
    - Sliced green onions

Instructions:

1. **Prepare the Base:** Cook your chosen base (brown rice, quinoa, or potatoes) according to package instructions. If using pre-cooked or leftover grains, reheat them as needed.
2. **Cook the Eggs:** Heat olive oil or butter in a non-stick skillet over medium heat. Crack the eggs into the skillet and scramble until fully cooked. Season with salt and pepper. You can also cook the eggs sunny-side up or over-easy if preferred.
3. **Assemble the Bowl:**
    - Start with a layer of your base in each bowl.
    - Top with the cooked beans.
    - Add the scrambled eggs on top.
    - Layer on the diced tomatoes, avocado, and shredded cheese.
4. **Add Toppings:**
    - Spoon salsa or pico de gallo over the top.
    - Garnish with fresh cilantro if using.
    - Serve with lime wedges for a squeeze of fresh lime juice.
5. **Optional Add-Ins:**
    - If desired, add sautéed bell peppers and onions for extra flavor.
    - Spice things up with sliced jalapeños or a drizzle of hot sauce.

6. **Serve:** Enjoy your Breakfast Burrito Bowl warm. Mix everything together or enjoy each component separately.

Tips

- **Customization:** Feel free to swap out or add ingredients based on your preferences or what you have on hand. For example, you can use sweet potatoes instead of regular potatoes, or add different vegetables.
- **Meal Prep:** This bowl is great for meal prep. You can prepare the base, beans, and toppings ahead of time and assemble the bowls as needed.
- **Cheese Options:** Experiment with different types of cheese or add a dollop of sour cream or Greek yogurt for extra creaminess.

Enjoy your Breakfast Burrito Bowl—it's a delicious and satisfying way to start your day!

Healthy Breakfast Cookies

Ingredients:

- 1 cup rolled oats
- 1/2 cup whole wheat flour (or use almond flour for a gluten-free option)
- 1/2 teaspoon baking powder
- 1/4 teaspoon salt
- 1/2 teaspoon ground cinnamon
- 1/4 cup coconut oil or unsalted butter, melted
- 1/4 cup honey or maple syrup
- 1 large ripe banana, mashed (about 1/2 cup)
- 1/4 cup nut butter (peanut butter, almond butter, or cashew butter)
- 1/2 cup add-ins (e.g., raisins, dried cranberries, dark chocolate chips, or nuts)
- Optional: 1/4 cup chia seeds or flaxseeds for added nutrition

Instructions:

1. **Preheat Oven:** Preheat your oven to 350°F (175°C). Line a baking sheet with parchment paper or a silicone baking mat.
2. **Mix Dry Ingredients:** In a large bowl, combine the rolled oats, whole wheat flour, baking powder, salt, and ground cinnamon.
3. **Mix Wet Ingredients:** In another bowl, whisk together the melted coconut oil or butter, honey or maple syrup, mashed banana, and nut butter until well combined.
4. **Combine Mixtures:** Pour the wet ingredients into the dry ingredients and stir until combined. Fold in your chosen add-ins and optional chia seeds or flaxseeds.
5. **Form Cookies:** Drop spoonfuls of dough onto the prepared baking sheet, flattening each slightly with the back of the spoon. The cookies won't spread much during baking, so shape them as you want them to look.
6. **Bake:** Bake in the preheated oven for 10-12 minutes, or until the cookies are golden brown around the edges and firm to the touch.
7. **Cool:** Allow the cookies to cool on the baking sheet for a few minutes before transferring them to a wire rack to cool completely.

Tips

- **Sweetener:** Adjust the sweetness by adding more or less honey or maple syrup according to your taste preference.
- **Add-Ins:** Feel free to mix and match your favorite add-ins like dried fruit, nuts, seeds, or chocolate chips.
- **Storage:** Store the cookies in an airtight container at room temperature for up to a week, or freeze them for longer storage. To freeze, place cookies in a single layer on a baking sheet and freeze until solid, then transfer to a zip-top bag or airtight container.

Enjoy your Healthy Breakfast Cookies—they're a perfect on-the-go option that's both satisfying and nutritious!

Granola and Fruit Parfait

Ingredients:

- 1 cup Greek yogurt (plain or vanilla, or use dairy-free yogurt if preferred)
- 1/2 cup granola (store-bought or homemade)
- 1 cup fresh fruit (e.g., berries, sliced banana, apple chunks, or kiwi)
- 1-2 tablespoons honey or maple syrup (optional, for added sweetness)
- A sprinkle of chia seeds or flaxseeds (optional)
- Fresh mint leaves for garnish (optional)

Instructions:

1. **Prepare Ingredients:** Wash and cut the fruit into bite-sized pieces if necessary. If using berries, you can leave them whole.
2. **Sweeten Yogurt (Optional):** If you prefer a sweeter yogurt, mix in 1-2 tablespoons of honey or maple syrup. Adjust the sweetness to your liking.
3. **Layer the Parfait:**
   - **First Layer:** Spoon a portion of Greek yogurt into the bottom of a glass or bowl.
   - **Second Layer:** Add a layer of granola on top of the yogurt.
   - **Third Layer:** Add a layer of fresh fruit on top of the granola.
4. **Repeat Layers:** Repeat the layers until you reach the top of the glass or bowl. Finish with a dollop of yogurt, a sprinkle of granola, and a few pieces of fruit on top.
5. **Add Optional Toppings:**
   - Sprinkle chia seeds or flaxseeds over the top for added nutrition.
   - Garnish with fresh mint leaves if desired.
6. **Serve:** Serve immediately or chill in the refrigerator for up to a few hours before serving.

Tips

- **Customization:** Feel free to customize your parfait with your favorite fruits and granola. You can also add a layer of nut butter or a drizzle of fruit compote for extra flavor.
- **Granola:** Choose granola that suits your taste preferences. You can use store-bought granola or make your own at home.
- **Yogurt:** For a dairy-free option, use coconut, almond, or soy yogurt.

Enjoy your Granola and Fruit Parfait—it's a delicious and satisfying way to enjoy a variety of textures and flavors in one bowl!

Scrambled Egg Tacos

Ingredients:

- 4 large eggs
- 1 tablespoon butter or olive oil
- Salt and pepper, to taste
- 4 small tortillas (corn or flour)
- 1/4 cup shredded cheese (cheddar, Monterey Jack, or your choice)
- 1/2 cup cooked black beans (optional)
- 1/2 cup diced tomatoes
- 1/4 cup finely chopped onion
- 1/4 cup chopped fresh cilantro (optional)
- 1 avocado, sliced
- Salsa or hot sauce, for serving
- Lime wedges, for garnish

Instructions:

1. **Prepare the Ingredients:**
    - Dice the tomatoes, chop the onion, and slice the avocado. If you're using black beans, warm them up.
2. **Scramble the Eggs:**
    - In a bowl, whisk the eggs with a pinch of salt and pepper.
    - Heat the butter or olive oil in a non-stick skillet over medium heat.
    - Pour the eggs into the skillet and cook, stirring gently with a spatula, until the eggs are fully cooked and scrambled. Remove from heat.
3. **Warm the Tortillas:**
    - Heat the tortillas in a dry skillet over medium heat, or warm them in the microwave. You can also wrap them in foil and warm them in the oven.
4. **Assemble the Tacos:**
    - Place a tortilla on a plate and spoon some scrambled eggs into the center.
    - Top with shredded cheese, cooked black beans (if using), diced tomatoes, chopped onion, and cilantro (if using).
    - Add slices of avocado.
5. **Add Salsa and Garnish:**
    - Spoon salsa or a drizzle of hot sauce over the top of the tacos.
    - Garnish with lime wedges for squeezing over the tacos.
6. **Serve:**
    - Serve the tacos warm, with extra lime wedges and salsa on the side.

Tips

- **Customization:** Feel free to add or substitute with other toppings like sautéed bell peppers, spinach, or mushrooms.
- **Cheese:** Choose a cheese that melts well if you want it to be extra gooey.
- **Beans:** If you're using canned beans, rinse them thoroughly and heat them before adding to the tacos.
- **Make-Ahead:** You can prepare the scrambled eggs and toppings in advance, and then quickly assemble the tacos when ready to eat.

Enjoy your Scrambled Egg Tacos—they're a delicious and satisfying meal that's easy to make and customize!

Peach Oat Bars

Ingredients:

- **For the Crust and Topping:**
    - 1 cup old-fashioned oats
    - 1/2 cup whole wheat flour (or all-purpose flour)
    - 1/2 cup coconut oil or unsalted butter, melted
    - 1/4 cup honey or maple syrup
    - 1/4 cup brown sugar or coconut sugar
    - 1/2 teaspoon ground cinnamon
    - 1/4 teaspoon salt
- **For the Peach Filling:**
    - 2 cups fresh peaches, peeled and diced (or use frozen peaches, thawed and drained)
    - 1/4 cup honey or maple syrup
    - 1 tablespoon cornstarch
    - 1/2 teaspoon vanilla extract
    - 1/4 teaspoon ground cinnamon (optional)

Instructions:

1. **Preheat Oven:** Preheat your oven to 350°F (175°C). Line an 8x8-inch baking pan with parchment paper or lightly grease it.
2. **Prepare the Crust and Topping:**
    - In a medium bowl, combine the oats, flour, melted coconut oil (or butter), honey (or maple syrup), brown sugar, ground cinnamon, and salt. Mix until well combined. The mixture should be crumbly.
3. **Press the Crust:**
    - Press about two-thirds of the oat mixture into the bottom of the prepared baking pan, creating an even layer. Set aside the remaining crumb mixture for the topping.
4. **Prepare the Peach Filling:**
    - In a medium saucepan, combine the diced peaches, honey (or maple syrup), cornstarch, vanilla extract, and ground cinnamon (if using). Cook over medium heat, stirring occasionally, until the mixture starts to thicken and bubble, about 5-7 minutes.
5. **Assemble the Bars:**
    - Pour the peach filling over the crust in the baking pan, spreading it evenly.
    - Sprinkle the reserved oat mixture evenly over the top of the peach filling.
6. **Bake:**
    - Bake in the preheated oven for 25-30 minutes, or until the topping is golden brown and the filling is bubbly.
7. **Cool and Slice:**

- Allow the bars to cool completely in the pan before lifting them out using the parchment paper (if used). Once cooled, cut into squares or bars.
8. **Serve:**
    - Serve at room temperature or chilled. Store any leftovers in an airtight container at room temperature for up to 3 days, or refrigerate for up to a week.

Tips

- **Peach Ripeness:** Use ripe peaches for the best flavor. If using frozen peaches, make sure to thaw and drain them well to avoid excess moisture.
- **Substitutions:** You can use other fruits such as blueberries, raspberries, or apples if peaches are not available.
- **Gluten-Free:** For a gluten-free version, use certified gluten-free oats and substitute the flour with a gluten-free blend.

Enjoy your Peach Oat Bars—a perfect blend of sweet, fruity, and wholesome goodness!

Homemade Breakfast Sausage Patties

Ingredients:

- 1 pound ground pork (or ground turkey for a leaner option)
- 1 teaspoon salt
- 1/2 teaspoon black pepper
- 1/2 teaspoon ground sage
- 1/2 teaspoon dried thyme
- 1/4 teaspoon crushed red pepper flakes (optional, for heat)
- 1/4 teaspoon garlic powder
- 1/4 teaspoon onion powder
- 1/4 teaspoon smoked paprika (optional, for a smoky flavor)
- 1 tablespoon maple syrup or honey (optional, for a touch of sweetness)
- 1 tablespoon fresh parsley, chopped (optional, for freshness)

Instructions:

1. **Prepare the Sausage Mixture:**
    - In a large bowl, combine the ground pork with salt, black pepper, sage, thyme, red pepper flakes (if using), garlic powder, onion powder, and smoked paprika (if using). If you like a bit of sweetness, mix in the maple syrup or honey. Add the fresh parsley if using.
    - Mix the ingredients until well combined. Be careful not to overmix, as this can make the patties tough.
2. **Form the Patties:**
    - Divide the sausage mixture into 8-10 equal portions (or more if you prefer smaller patties). Shape each portion into a patty, about 1/2 inch thick. You can use your hands or a burger press for more uniform patties.
3. **Cook the Patties:**
    - Heat a skillet or griddle over medium heat. You don't need additional oil if using a non-stick skillet, as the fat from the sausage will be sufficient.
    - Cook the patties for about 4-5 minutes per side, or until they are well-browned and cooked through to an internal temperature of 160°F (71°C). You can use a meat thermometer to check for doneness.
4. **Serve:**
    - Serve the sausage patties hot. They are great on their own or with eggs, in a breakfast sandwich, or as part of a breakfast platter.
5. **Store and Freeze:**
    - **To Store:** Keep any leftover patties in an airtight container in the refrigerator for up to 4 days.
    - **To Freeze:** Let the cooked patties cool completely, then place them in a single layer on a baking sheet to freeze. Once frozen, transfer the patties to a zip-top bag or airtight container. Reheat from frozen in a skillet or microwave.

Tips

- **Spice Levels:** Adjust the amount of red pepper flakes and seasoning based on your preference for spice and flavor.
- **Lean Meat:** If using lean ground turkey, you may need to add a bit of oil to the pan to prevent sticking, as it has less fat than pork.
- **Fresh Herbs:** Fresh herbs like parsley or thyme can be substituted for dried herbs if you have them on hand.

Enjoy your Homemade Breakfast Sausage Patties—they're a delicious and satisfying addition to any breakfast!

Berry Muffins

Ingredients:

- 1 1/2 cups all-purpose flour
- 1/2 cup whole wheat flour (optional, for added nutrition)
- 1 cup granulated sugar
- 1 tablespoon baking powder
- 1/2 teaspoon salt
- 1/2 cup unsalted butter, melted
- 2 large eggs
- 1 cup milk (whole milk or a dairy-free alternative)
- 1 teaspoon vanilla extract
- 1 1/2 cups mixed berries (fresh or frozen; e.g., blueberries, raspberries, blackberries, or chopped strawberries)
- Optional: 1 tablespoon coarse sugar for topping

Instructions:

1. **Preheat Oven:** Preheat your oven to 375°F (190°C). Line a 12-cup muffin tin with paper liners or lightly grease the cups.
2. **Mix Dry Ingredients:** In a large bowl, whisk together the all-purpose flour, whole wheat flour (if using), sugar, baking powder, and salt.
3. **Mix Wet Ingredients:** In a separate bowl, whisk together the melted butter, eggs, milk, and vanilla extract.
4. **Combine Mixtures:** Pour the wet ingredients into the dry ingredients and stir until just combined. Be careful not to overmix; the batter should be a bit lumpy.
5. **Fold in Berries:** Gently fold in the berries. If using frozen berries, do not thaw them to prevent the batter from turning too colorful.
6. **Fill Muffin Cups:** Divide the batter evenly among the 12 muffin cups. If desired, sprinkle the tops with coarse sugar for a crunchy, sweet finish.
7. **Bake:** Bake in the preheated oven for 18-22 minutes, or until the muffins are golden brown and a toothpick inserted into the center comes out clean.
8. **Cool:** Allow the muffins to cool in the pan for about 5 minutes before transferring them to a wire rack to cool completely.

Tips

- **Berry Variations:** Feel free to use a single type of berry or a mix of your favorites. If using larger berries like strawberries, cut them into smaller pieces to ensure even distribution.
- **Gluten-Free Option:** Substitute the all-purpose flour with a gluten-free flour blend if needed.

- **Storage:** Store muffins in an airtight container at room temperature for up to 3 days, or freeze them for up to 3 months. To freeze, place muffins in a zip-top bag or airtight container and thaw at room temperature or microwave before serving.

Enjoy your Berry Muffins—they're a sweet and nutritious way to brighten up your morning or enjoy as a tasty snack!

Spinach and Feta Egg Bites

Ingredients:

- 6 large eggs
- 1 cup fresh spinach, chopped
- 1/2 cup crumbled feta cheese
- 1/4 cup milk (any kind you prefer)
- 1/4 cup grated Parmesan cheese (optional)
- 1/4 teaspoon garlic powder (optional)
- 1/4 teaspoon onion powder (optional)
- Salt and pepper, to taste
- Cooking spray or a bit of oil, for greasing

Instructions:

1. **Preheat the Oven**: Set your oven to 375°F (190°C). Grease a muffin tin with cooking spray or lightly oil it.
2. **Prepare the Spinach**: If you're using fresh spinach, chop it and then lightly sauté it in a pan over medium heat until wilted (about 2-3 minutes). You can skip this step if you prefer a fresher taste or are using pre-cooked spinach.
3. **Mix the Ingredients**: In a large bowl, whisk together the eggs, milk, and a pinch of salt and pepper. If using, add the garlic powder and onion powder. Stir in the chopped spinach and crumbled feta cheese (and Parmesan if using).
4. **Fill the Muffin Tin**: Pour the egg mixture evenly into the muffin tin cups, filling them about 3/4 full.
5. **Bake**: Place the muffin tin in the preheated oven and bake for about 20-25 minutes, or until the egg bites are set and slightly golden on top. A toothpick inserted into the center should come out clean.
6. **Cool and Serve**: Let the egg bites cool in the tin for a few minutes before removing them. Serve warm or at room temperature.

Tips:

- **Add-ins**: You can customize these bites by adding other ingredients like diced bell peppers, onions, or cooked bacon.
- **Storage**: Store leftover egg bites in an airtight container in the refrigerator for up to a week. They can also be frozen for up to 3 months. Reheat them in the microwave or oven.

Enjoy your spinach and feta egg bites! They're great for meal prep and easy to grab on the go.

Cream Cheese and Jelly Bagels

Ingredients:

- **4 bagels** (any flavor you like)
- **4 oz cream cheese** (softened)
- **1/4 cup jelly or jam** (your choice of flavor, such as strawberry, grape, or raspberry)
- **Optional toppings**: fresh fruit slices, a sprinkle of nuts, or a drizzle of honey

Instructions:

1. **Toast the Bagels**: Slice the bagels in half and toast them to your desired level of crispiness.
2. **Prepare the Cream Cheese**: While the bagels are toasting, spread the softened cream cheese evenly on each bagel half.
3. **Add the Jelly**: Spoon a generous amount of jelly or jam over the cream cheese. You can spread it out evenly or leave it in dollops, depending on your preference.
4. **Optional Toppings**: If you want to add extra flair, consider topping the bagels with fresh fruit slices (like strawberries or bananas), a sprinkle of nuts (like chopped almonds or walnuts), or a light drizzle of honey.
5. **Serve**: Enjoy the bagels immediately while they're fresh and the cream cheese is creamy.

Tips:

- **Cream Cheese Variations**: You can use flavored cream cheese if you want to experiment with different tastes. For example, chive cream cheese pairs well with fruitier jams.
- **Homemade Bagels**: If you're feeling ambitious, you can make your own bagels from scratch for an even more delicious treat.
- **Serving Suggestion**: These bagels make a great breakfast or a sweet snack. They're also fun to serve at brunches or casual get-togethers.

Enjoy your cream cheese and jelly bagels! They're a quick and tasty way to satisfy a sweet craving.

Mini Pancake Skewers

Ingredients:

For the Mini Pancakes:

- 1 cup all-purpose flour
- 2 tablespoons sugar
- 1 tablespoon baking powder
- 1/2 teaspoon salt
- 1 cup milk
- 1 large egg
- 2 tablespoons melted butter or vegetable oil
- Butter or oil, for cooking

For the Skewers:

- **Fresh fruit** (such as strawberries, blueberries, bananas, or apple slices)
- **Maple syrup**, **honey**, or **chocolate sauce** for dipping
- **Powdered sugar** or **whipped cream** (optional, for serving)

Instructions:

1. **Prepare the Pancake Batter**: In a medium bowl, whisk together the flour, sugar, baking powder, and salt. In another bowl, mix the milk, egg, and melted butter or oil. Combine the wet and dry ingredients, stirring until just combined. The batter will be slightly lumpy, which is fine.
2. **Cook the Mini Pancakes**: Heat a non-stick skillet or griddle over medium heat and lightly grease it with butter or oil. Use a tablespoon or a mini ice cream scoop to drop small amounts of batter onto the skillet, creating mini pancakes. Cook until bubbles form on the surface and the edges look set, then flip and cook for another 1-2 minutes until golden brown. Repeat with the remaining batter.
3. **Assemble the Skewers**: Once the mini pancakes are cooked, let them cool slightly. Thread the mini pancakes onto small skewers or toothpicks, alternating with pieces of fresh fruit.
4. **Serve**: Arrange the skewers on a platter and serve with your choice of dipping sauces like maple syrup, honey, or chocolate sauce. You can also dust them with powdered sugar or serve with a dollop of whipped cream if desired.

Tips:

- **Variations**: You can add chocolate chips or blueberries to the pancake batter for extra flavor.

- **Make-Ahead**: You can cook the mini pancakes ahead of time and keep them warm in the oven (set to a low temperature) until you're ready to assemble the skewers.
- **Creative Additions**: Consider adding small pieces of cooked bacon or sausage between the pancakes for a savory twist.

These mini pancake skewers are sure to be a hit with kids and adults alike! Enjoy the fun and tasty presentation.

Breakfast Smoothie

Ingredients:

- **1 cup milk** (dairy or non-dairy like almond, soy, or oat milk)
- **1 banana** (fresh or frozen)
- **1/2 cup Greek yogurt** (plain or vanilla)
- **1/2 cup frozen berries** (such as blueberries, strawberries, or mixed berries)
- **1 tablespoon honey or maple syrup** (optional, for added sweetness)
- **1 tablespoon chia seeds or flaxseeds** (optional, for extra fiber and omega-3s)
- **A handful of spinach** (optional, for added nutrients)

Instructions:

1. **Blend Ingredients**: In a blender, combine the milk, banana, Greek yogurt, frozen berries, and any optional ingredients you're using.
2. **Blend Until Smooth**: Blend on high speed until all ingredients are well combined and the smoothie is smooth and creamy.
3. **Taste and Adjust**: Taste the smoothie and adjust sweetness if needed by adding honey or maple syrup. If the smoothie is too thick, you can add a little more milk to reach your desired consistency.
4. **Serve**: Pour into a glass and enjoy immediately. You can also pour it into a travel cup if you're on the go.

Customization Ideas:

- **Protein Boost**: Add a scoop of protein powder, or a tablespoon of nut butter (like almond or peanut butter) for extra protein.
- **Fruits and Veggies**: Swap out the frozen berries for other fruits like mango, pineapple, or peaches. You can also add other veggies like kale or cucumber for a different nutrient profile.
- **Flavor Enhancements**: Add a pinch of cinnamon, vanilla extract, or a tablespoon of cocoa powder for added flavor.
- **Superfoods**: Incorporate superfoods like spirulina, matcha powder, or a handful of nuts and seeds for additional health benefits.

Tips:

- **Frozen Fruit**: Using frozen fruit helps make the smoothie thicker and colder. If you're using fresh fruit, you might want to add a handful of ice cubes.
- **Make Ahead**: You can prepare smoothie packs by portioning out fruits, veggies, and seeds into freezer bags. When you're ready to make a smoothie, just dump a pack into the blender with your liquid.

Enjoy your breakfast smoothie! It's a great way to pack in nutrients and get your day started on the right foot.

Pumpkin Spice Oatmeal

Ingredients:

- **1 cup rolled oats**
- **1 cup milk** (dairy or non-dairy like almond, soy, or oat milk)
- **1/2 cup canned pumpkin** (not pumpkin pie filling, just pure pumpkin)
- **1 tablespoon brown sugar** (or maple syrup, honey, or your preferred sweetener)
- **1/2 teaspoon pumpkin pie spice** (or a mix of cinnamon, nutmeg, ginger, and cloves)
- **1/4 teaspoon vanilla extract**
- **Pinch of salt**
- **Optional toppings**: chopped nuts (like pecans or walnuts), dried cranberries, a dollop of Greek yogurt, extra pumpkin pie spice, or a drizzle of maple syrup

Instructions:

1. **Combine Ingredients**: In a medium saucepan, combine the rolled oats, milk, canned pumpkin, brown sugar, pumpkin pie spice, vanilla extract, and a pinch of salt.
2. **Cook the Oatmeal**: Bring the mixture to a boil over medium-high heat, then reduce the heat to low. Simmer, stirring occasionally, for about 5-7 minutes, or until the oats are tender and the mixture has thickened to your liking.
3. **Serve**: Spoon the oatmeal into bowls and add your favorite toppings if desired.
4. **Enjoy**: Serve warm and enjoy your pumpkin spice oatmeal!

Tips:

- **Texture Adjustment**: For creamier oatmeal, you can use all milk instead of a mix of water and milk, or add a bit more milk if you prefer a looser consistency.
- **Make Ahead**: You can prepare this oatmeal in advance and store it in the refrigerator for up to 3-4 days. Reheat it in the microwave or on the stovetop, adding a little extra milk if needed.
- **Pumpkin Purée**: If you have leftover pumpkin purée, you can freeze it in ice cube trays and then transfer the cubes to a freezer bag. This way, you can easily use a few cubes in future oatmeal recipes.

Pumpkin spice oatmeal is a wonderful way to enjoy the flavors of fall any time of the year. It's nutritious, filling, and can be customized to suit your taste!

Almond Butter Apple Sandwiches

Ingredients:

- **1 large apple** (any variety you prefer, such as Honeycrisp, Fuji, or Gala)
- **1/4 cup almond butter** (or any nut or seed butter of your choice)
- **1 tablespoon honey** (optional, for extra sweetness)
- **A pinch of cinnamon** (optional, for added flavor)
- **Granola** or **raisins** (optional, for added texture and sweetness)

Instructions:

1. **Prepare the Apple**: Wash and core the apple. Slice it into thin, even rounds. If you want to prevent browning, you can sprinkle the slices with a bit of lemon juice.
2. **Spread the Almond Butter**: Spread a layer of almond butter on one side of each apple slice. If you like a little extra sweetness, drizzle a small amount of honey over the almond butter.
3. **Add Extras**: If you're using cinnamon, sprinkle a little on top of the almond butter. For added texture, you can sprinkle some granola or raisins on the almond butter before placing the other apple slice on top.
4. **Assemble the Sandwiches**: Top each almond butter-spread apple slice with another apple slice to form a sandwich. Press down gently to help everything stick together.
5. **Serve**: Enjoy immediately, or pack them for a snack later in the day.

Tips:

- **Variations**: Try different nut butters, such as peanut butter or cashew butter, for a change. You can also use different types of apples to find your favorite combination.
- **Nut-Free Option**: For a nut-free version, use sunflower seed butter or another nut-free spread.
- **Presentation**: For a fun presentation, you can cut the apple slices into fun shapes using cookie cutters.

These almond butter apple sandwiches are not only tasty but also packed with nutrients. They make for a great snack for kids and adults alike, providing a good balance of protein, fiber, and healthy fats.

Breakfast Tostadas

Ingredients:

- 4 small corn or flour tortillas
- 1 tablespoon olive oil (or any cooking oil of your choice)
- 4 large eggs
- 1/2 cup black beans (canned or cooked, drained and rinsed)
- 1/2 cup shredded cheese (such as cheddar, Monterey Jack, or queso fresco)
- 1/2 avocado, sliced
- 1/4 cup salsa (store-bought or homemade)
- Salt and pepper, to taste
- Optional garnishes: chopped cilantro, sliced green onions, sour cream, or hot sauce

Instructions:

1. **Prepare the Tortillas**: Preheat your oven to 400°F (200°C). Brush both sides of the tortillas with olive oil and place them on a baking sheet. Bake for 5-7 minutes, or until they're crispy and golden. You can also crisp them up in a skillet over medium heat if you prefer.
2. **Cook the Eggs**: While the tortillas are baking, heat a non-stick skillet over medium heat. Scramble the eggs in a bowl and pour them into the skillet. Cook, stirring occasionally, until the eggs are fully cooked. Season with salt and pepper.
3. **Warm the Beans**: In a small saucepan, heat the black beans over medium heat until warm. You can season them with a bit of cumin, garlic powder, or chili powder if you like.
4. **Assemble the Tostadas**: Once the tortillas are crispy, remove them from the oven. Spread a layer of black beans over each tostada. Top with scrambled eggs and shredded cheese. Return to the oven for another 2-3 minutes to melt the cheese, or use the broiler for a quick melt.
5. **Add Toppings**: Remove from the oven and add avocado slices, salsa, and any optional garnishes you like.
6. **Serve**: Serve immediately while the tostadas are still warm and crispy.

Customization Ideas:

- **Meat Additions**: Add cooked bacon, sausage, or chorizo for a heartier option.
- **Vegetables**: Include sautéed bell peppers, onions, or spinach for extra veggies.
- **Spicy Kick**: Add jalapeño slices or a drizzle of hot sauce for some heat.
- **Salsa Variations**: Experiment with different types of salsa, like roasted tomato salsa, verde salsa, or pico de gallo.

Tips:

- **Make Ahead**: You can prep the components ahead of time and assemble the tostadas quickly in the morning.
- **Texture**: For extra crunch, try toasting the tortillas a little longer or using a thicker tortilla.

Breakfast tostadas are incredibly versatile and can be adapted to fit various tastes and dietary preferences. Enjoy crafting your perfect tostada!

Fruit Salad with Honey Lime Dressing

Ingredients:

For the Fruit Salad:

- **1 cup strawberries**, hulled and sliced
- **1 cup blueberries**
- **1 cup grapes**, halved if large
- **1 cup pineapple**, cut into bite-sized chunks
- **1 cup kiwi**, peeled and sliced
- **1 orange**, peeled and segmented
- **1 apple**, cored and diced (optional)

For the Honey Lime Dressing:

- **1/4 cup honey**
- **2 tablespoons fresh lime juice**
- **1 teaspoon lime zest**
- **1/2 teaspoon vanilla extract** (optional)

Instructions:

1. **Prepare the Fruit**: Wash and cut all the fruit as needed. In a large mixing bowl, combine the strawberries, blueberries, grapes, pineapple, kiwi, orange segments, and apple (if using).
2. **Make the Dressing**: In a small bowl, whisk together the honey, lime juice, lime zest, and vanilla extract (if using). Taste and adjust sweetness or acidity as needed.
3. **Toss the Salad**: Drizzle the honey lime dressing over the fruit and gently toss to coat everything evenly.
4. **Chill**: For the best flavor, cover the fruit salad and let it chill in the refrigerator for at least 30 minutes before serving. This allows the flavors to meld together.
5. **Serve**: Serve the fruit salad chilled.

Tips:

- **Fruit Variety**: Feel free to mix and match fruits based on what's in season or what you have on hand. Other good options include mangoes, raspberries, or pomegranate seeds.
- **Freshness**: For the freshest taste, prepare the fruit salad and dressing shortly before serving.
- **Adjust Sweetness**: If you prefer a less sweet dressing, you can reduce the amount of honey or add a little more lime juice.

This fruit salad with honey lime dressing is perfect for summer gatherings, brunches, or as a healthy snack. It's vibrant, refreshing, and packed with natural sweetness!

Cheesy Spinach Stuffed Biscuits

Ingredients:

For the Biscuit Dough:

- 2 1/4 cups all-purpose flour
- 1 tablespoon baking powder
- 1/2 teaspoon salt
- 1/2 teaspoon baking soda
- 1/2 cup cold butter, cut into small pieces
- 1 cup buttermilk (or milk with 1 tablespoon lemon juice or vinegar, let sit for 5 minutes)

For the Spinach Filling:

- 1 cup fresh spinach, chopped (or 1/2 cup frozen spinach, thawed and squeezed dry)
- 1/2 cup shredded cheese (cheddar, mozzarella, or your choice)
- 1/4 cup cream cheese, softened
- 1 clove garlic, minced (optional)
- Salt and pepper, to taste

Instructions:

1. **Preheat the Oven**: Set your oven to 425°F (220°C). Line a baking sheet with parchment paper or lightly grease it.
2. **Prepare the Biscuit Dough**:
    - In a large bowl, whisk together the flour, baking powder, salt, and baking soda.
    - Cut the cold butter into the flour mixture using a pastry cutter, fork, or your fingers until the mixture resembles coarse crumbs.
    - Gradually add the buttermilk, stirring until the dough just comes together. Avoid overmixing.
3. **Prepare the Spinach Filling**:
    - In a medium bowl, combine the chopped spinach, shredded cheese, cream cheese, and minced garlic (if using). Season with salt and pepper to taste.
4. **Assemble the Biscuits**:
    - On a lightly floured surface, roll out the biscuit dough into a rectangle about 1/2 inch thick.
    - Spread the spinach mixture evenly over one half of the dough.
    - Fold the other half of the dough over the filling and press down gently to seal.
5. **Cut and Bake**:
    - Use a biscuit cutter or a knife to cut the dough into squares or circles, depending on your preference.
    - Place the cut biscuits onto the prepared baking sheet.
    - Bake for 12-15 minutes, or until the biscuits are golden brown and cooked through.

6. **Serve**:
    - Allow the biscuits to cool slightly before serving.

Tips:

- **Freezing**: You can freeze the unbaked stuffed biscuits on a baking sheet, then transfer them to a freezer bag for future use. Bake from frozen, adding a few extra minutes to the baking time.
- **Flavor Variations**: Feel free to add herbs like dill or thyme to the filling for extra flavor.
- **Dough Alternatives**: You can use store-bought biscuit dough if you prefer a quicker option. Just roll it out and follow the same steps for filling and baking.

These cheesy spinach stuffed biscuits are sure to be a hit with their flaky, buttery crust and savory, cheesy filling. Enjoy them fresh from the oven for the best taste!

Sweet Potato Hash Browns

Ingredients:

- 2 large sweet potatoes, peeled
- 1 small onion, finely chopped
- 2 cloves garlic, minced
- 1/4 cup flour (all-purpose or a gluten-free alternative)
- 1 large egg
- 1/2 teaspoon paprika
- 1/4 teaspoon ground cumin
- Salt and pepper, to taste
- 2 tablespoons olive oil (or another cooking oil of your choice)

Instructions:

1. **Prepare the Sweet Potatoes**:
   - Grate the peeled sweet potatoes using a box grater or a food processor fitted with a grating attachment.
   - Place the grated sweet potatoes in a clean kitchen towel or cheesecloth and squeeze out as much moisture as possible. This step is crucial for achieving crispiness.
2. **Mix the Ingredients**:
   - In a large bowl, combine the grated sweet potatoes, chopped onion, minced garlic, flour, egg, paprika, cumin, salt, and pepper. Mix well until all ingredients are evenly distributed.
3. **Heat the Oil**:
   - Heat the olive oil in a large skillet over medium heat. You want enough oil to cover the bottom of the skillet.
4. **Cook the Hash Browns**:
   - Take about 1/4 cup of the sweet potato mixture and press it into a patty shape. Place it in the hot skillet. Repeat with the remaining mixture, making sure not to overcrowd the skillet.
   - Cook each patty for 4-5 minutes per side, or until golden brown and crispy. Flip carefully using a spatula.
5. **Drain and Serve**:
   - Transfer the cooked hash browns to a paper towel-lined plate to drain any excess oil. Serve immediately.

Tips:

- **Consistency**: If the mixture feels too wet, add a little more flour. It should hold together well but still be easy to form into patties.

- **Flavor Variations**: Feel free to add spices or herbs like chopped parsley, chives, or a pinch of cayenne pepper for extra flavor.
- **Batch Cooking**: You can make these ahead of time and reheat them in a skillet to regain their crispiness.

Sweet potato hash browns are perfect for breakfast, brunch, or as a tasty side dish. Enjoy them with eggs, avocado, or your favorite dipping sauce!

Baked Eggs in Avocado

Ingredients:

- 2 ripe avocados
- 4 large eggs
- Salt and pepper, to taste
- 1/4 teaspoon paprika (optional)
- 1/4 teaspoon garlic powder (optional)
- 1/4 cup shredded cheese (optional, such as cheddar, feta, or mozzarella)
- Fresh herbs (optional, such as chives, parsley, or cilantro, for garnish)
- Red pepper flakes (optional, for a bit of heat)

Instructions:

1. **Preheat the Oven**: Set your oven to 425°F (220°C).
2. **Prepare the Avocados**:
   - Cut the avocados in half and remove the pit. If the indent where the pit was is too small to hold an egg, scoop out a little extra flesh to create more space. Be careful not to scoop too much, or the avocado may collapse.
3. **Prepare the Baking Sheet**:
   - Place the avocado halves in a baking dish or on a baking sheet. If the avocados wobble or don't sit flat, you can place them in a muffin tin or use crumpled foil to stabilize them.
4. **Add the Eggs**:
   - Carefully crack an egg into a small bowl and gently slide it into the well of each avocado half. Repeat with the remaining eggs, making sure not to overflow the avocado.
5. **Season and Bake**:
   - Season each avocado with salt, pepper, paprika, and garlic powder. If using cheese, sprinkle it on top of the eggs.
   - Bake for 12-15 minutes, or until the egg whites are set but the yolks are still slightly runny (or cooked to your desired consistency). The baking time may vary depending on the size of the eggs and avocados.
6. **Garnish and Serve**:
   - Remove from the oven and let cool slightly. Garnish with fresh herbs and red pepper flakes if desired.
   - Serve immediately, with a side of toast, or as part of a larger meal.

Tips:

- **Texture Preference**: If you prefer a firmer yolk, bake for a few extra minutes. If you want to ensure the yolk remains runny, start checking at around 10 minutes.

- **Add-ins**: Feel free to add other ingredients to the avocado before baking, such as cooked bacon, sautéed spinach, or a few cherry tomato halves.
- **Adjusting Size**: If your avocado halves are particularly small or large, adjust the number of eggs or their size accordingly.

Baked eggs in avocado are a nutritious, low-carb option that's both satisfying and delicious. Enjoy this dish fresh out of the oven for the best texture and flavor!

Whole Wheat Waffles

Ingredients:

- 1 3/4 cups whole wheat flour
- 1 tablespoon baking powder
- 1/2 teaspoon baking soda
- 1/2 teaspoon salt
- 2 tablespoons honey (or maple syrup, or your preferred sweetener)
- 1 1/2 cups buttermilk (or milk with 1 tablespoon lemon juice or vinegar, let sit for 5 minutes)
- 1/2 cup plain Greek yogurt (or regular yogurt)
- 2 large eggs
- 1/4 cup melted coconut oil (or butter, or another cooking oil)
- 1 teaspoon vanilla extract

Instructions:

1. **Preheat the Waffle Iron**: Preheat your waffle iron according to the manufacturer's instructions.
2. **Prepare the Dry Ingredients**: In a large bowl, whisk together the whole wheat flour, baking powder, baking soda, and salt.
3. **Mix the Wet Ingredients**: In a separate bowl, mix the honey, buttermilk, Greek yogurt, eggs, melted coconut oil, and vanilla extract until well combined.
4. **Combine**: Pour the wet ingredients into the dry ingredients and stir until just combined. The batter may be a bit lumpy, which is fine. Avoid overmixing.
5. **Cook the Waffles**: Lightly grease the waffle iron with cooking spray or brush with a small amount of oil. Pour the recommended amount of batter onto the preheated waffle iron (amount varies depending on the size of your waffle iron). Close the lid and cook according to the manufacturer's instructions, usually for about 3-5 minutes, or until the waffles are golden brown and crisp.
6. **Serve**: Remove the waffles and serve immediately with your favorite toppings.

Topping Ideas:

- **Fresh Fruit**: Top with berries, banana slices, or apple chunks.
- **Nuts and Seeds**: Sprinkle with chopped nuts or seeds for added crunch.
- **Yogurt or Whipped Cream**: Add a dollop of Greek yogurt or whipped cream.
- **Syrups and Spreads**: Drizzle with maple syrup, honey, or nut butter.

Tips:

- **Make-Ahead**: You can make a batch of waffles ahead of time and freeze them. To reheat, toast them in a toaster or oven to regain their crispiness.

- **Adjust Sweetness**: If you prefer sweeter waffles, you can increase the amount of honey or add a bit of brown sugar.
- **Flavor Variations**: Add spices like cinnamon or nutmeg to the batter for extra flavor, or mix in some chocolate chips or dried fruit.

Whole wheat waffles are a wholesome, tasty breakfast option that pairs well with a variety of toppings. Enjoy them fresh and warm for the best texture and flavor!

Breakfast Quesadilla Roll-Ups

Ingredients:

- 4 large flour tortillas (or whole wheat tortillas)
- 1 cup shredded cheese (such as cheddar, Monterey Jack, or a blend)
- 4 large eggs
- 1/4 cup milk (or cream)
- 1/2 cup cooked and crumbled breakfast sausage (or bacon, ham, or vegetarian option)
- 1/4 cup finely chopped onion (optional)
- 1/4 cup diced bell pepper (optional)
- 1/4 cup salsa (optional)
- Salt and pepper, to taste
- 1 tablespoon butter (for cooking)

Instructions:

1. **Prepare the Eggs**:
    - In a bowl, whisk together the eggs, milk, salt, and pepper. Heat a non-stick skillet over medium heat and melt a small amount of butter.
    - Pour in the egg mixture and cook, stirring occasionally, until the eggs are fully scrambled and cooked through. Set aside.
2. **Prepare the Tortillas**:
    - Lay out the tortillas and sprinkle a layer of shredded cheese on each one. Add the cooked eggs, crumbled sausage, and any optional ingredients like onion or bell pepper. If using salsa, you can either add it directly to the tortillas or serve it on the side.
3. **Roll Up the Tortillas**:
    - Roll each tortilla up tightly, like a cigar, to create a log shape.
4. **Cook the Roll-Ups**:
    - Heat a skillet over medium heat and melt a bit of butter. Place the rolled tortillas seam side down in the skillet and cook for 1-2 minutes on each side, or until they are golden brown and the cheese is melted. You can also use a griddle for multiple roll-ups at once.
5. **Serve**:
    - Slice the roll-ups into bite-sized pieces and serve warm. They can be enjoyed on their own or with a side of salsa, sour cream, or guacamole.

Tips:

- **Make-Ahead**: You can prepare the roll-ups ahead of time and freeze them. To reheat, simply microwave or toast them until heated through.
- **Flavor Variations**: Experiment with different cheeses, meats, or vegetables. For a spicy kick, add some jalapeño or hot sauce.

- **Vegetarian Option**: Skip the meat and add more veggies, such as mushrooms, spinach, or tomatoes.

These breakfast quesadilla roll-ups are versatile and can be customized to suit your tastes. They're perfect for busy mornings, brunch gatherings, or even as a fun snack!

Berry Chia Jam Toast

Ingredients:

For the Berry Chia Jam:

- 2 cups mixed berries (fresh or frozen; strawberries, blueberries, raspberries, or blackberries)
- 2 tablespoons honey (or maple syrup, agave nectar, or your preferred sweetener)
- 2 tablespoons chia seeds
- 1 tablespoon lemon juice (optional, for added flavor)
- 1/2 teaspoon vanilla extract (optional)

For the Toast:

- **4 slices of whole grain or sourdough bread**
- **Butter or coconut oil** (for toasting, optional)

Instructions:

1. **Make the Berry Chia Jam**:
   - In a medium saucepan, combine the berries and honey. Cook over medium heat, stirring occasionally, until the berries break down and the mixture starts to bubble, about 5-7 minutes.
   - Use a fork or potato masher to mash the berries to your desired consistency.
   - Stir in the chia seeds and continue to cook for another 2-3 minutes. The chia seeds will absorb liquid and thicken the jam.
   - Remove from heat and stir in the lemon juice and vanilla extract if using. Let the jam cool to room temperature; it will continue to thicken as it cools. Transfer to a jar or container and refrigerate. The jam can be stored in the refrigerator for up to 2 weeks.
2. **Prepare the Toast**:
   - Toast the bread slices in a toaster or on a skillet until crispy and golden brown. If you prefer, you can spread a thin layer of butter or coconut oil on the bread before toasting.
3. **Assemble and Serve**:
   - Spread a generous amount of berry chia jam over each slice of toasted bread.
   - Optionally, you can garnish with additional fresh berries or a sprinkle of chia seeds for extra texture.

Tips:

- **Adjust Sweetness**: Feel free to adjust the amount of honey or sweetener to suit your taste. You can also add a touch of cinnamon or nutmeg to the jam for extra flavor.

- **Berry Combinations**: Experiment with different combinations of berries or even try adding a small amount of fruit like mango or peach for a different twist.
- **Serving Suggestions**: This jam is also great as a topping for yogurt, pancakes, waffles, or as a filling for pastries.

Berry chia jam toast is a delightful and wholesome breakfast that combines the freshness of berries with the crunch of toast and the added nutritional benefits of chia seeds. Enjoy it fresh and warm for the best taste!

Oatmeal Breakfast Bars

Ingredients:

- 2 cups old-fashioned rolled oats
- 1/2 cup almond butter (or peanut butter, cashew butter, or any nut/seed butter)
- 1/2 cup honey (or maple syrup, agave nectar)
- 1/2 cup mashed banana (about 1 medium banana, or you can use applesauce)
- 1/2 cup dried fruit (such as raisins, cranberries, or chopped dates)
- 1/4 cup chopped nuts (such as almonds, walnuts, or pecans)
- 1/2 teaspoon cinnamon (optional)
- 1/4 teaspoon salt
- 1/4 cup mini chocolate chips (optional, for added sweetness)

Instructions:

1. **Preheat the Oven**: Preheat your oven to 350°F (175°C). Line an 8x8-inch baking pan with parchment paper or lightly grease it.
2. **Prepare the Wet Ingredients**:
   - In a medium saucepan, heat the almond butter and honey over low heat until melted and combined. Remove from heat and stir in the mashed banana.
3. **Combine Dry Ingredients**:
   - In a large bowl, mix the oats, dried fruit, chopped nuts, cinnamon, and salt.
4. **Mix Everything Together**:
   - Pour the wet mixture over the dry ingredients and stir until well combined. If you're adding chocolate chips, fold them in at this stage.
5. **Press into Pan**:
   - Transfer the mixture to the prepared baking pan. Use a spatula or the back of a spoon to press it down evenly and firmly.
6. **Bake**:
   - Bake for 20-25 minutes, or until the edges are golden brown and the center is set. The bars will firm up as they cool.
7. **Cool and Cut**:
   - Allow the bars to cool completely in the pan before lifting them out using the parchment paper. Cut into squares or bars.
8. **Store**:
   - Store the bars in an airtight container at room temperature for up to a week, or in the refrigerator for longer freshness.

Tips:

- **Customizations**: Feel free to add different mix-ins such as seeds (chia, flax, or pumpkin seeds), coconut flakes, or protein powder to boost the nutritional value.
- **Sweetness**: Adjust the amount of honey or sweetener to your taste preference.

- **Texture**: For chewier bars, use more banana or applesauce. For crunchier bars, increase the amount of nuts or add a bit of extra oats.

These oatmeal breakfast bars are versatile and can be tailored to fit your dietary preferences and taste. Enjoy them as a quick breakfast, a snack, or even a light dessert!

Zucchini Bread Muffins

Ingredients:

- 1 1/2 cups all-purpose flour (or whole wheat flour for added nutrition)
- 1/2 cup granulated sugar (or a mix of granulated and brown sugar)
- 1/4 cup brown sugar (optional, for added moisture and flavor)
- 1 teaspoon baking powder
- 1/2 teaspoon baking soda
- 1/2 teaspoon salt
- 1 teaspoon ground cinnamon
- 1/2 teaspoon ground nutmeg (optional)
- 1/2 cup vegetable oil (or melted coconut oil)
- 2 large eggs
- 1 teaspoon vanilla extract
- 1 1/2 cups grated zucchini (about 1 medium zucchini, unpeeled)
- 1/2 cup chopped nuts (such as walnuts or pecans, optional)
- 1/2 cup chocolate chips (optional, for a bit of sweetness)

Instructions:

1. **Preheat the Oven**: Preheat your oven to 350°F (175°C). Line a muffin tin with paper liners or lightly grease it.
2. **Prepare the Zucchini**:
    - Grate the zucchini and place it in a clean kitchen towel or cheesecloth. Squeeze out as much moisture as possible. This step helps prevent the muffins from becoming too soggy.
3. **Mix Dry Ingredients**:
    - In a large bowl, whisk together the flour, granulated sugar, brown sugar (if using), baking powder, baking soda, salt, cinnamon, and nutmeg.
4. **Mix Wet Ingredients**:
    - In another bowl, whisk together the oil, eggs, and vanilla extract. Stir in the grated zucchini.
5. **Combine Wet and Dry Ingredients**:
    - Add the wet ingredients to the dry ingredients and stir until just combined. Be careful not to overmix. Fold in the nuts and chocolate chips if using.
6. **Fill Muffin Tin**:
    - Divide the batter evenly among the muffin cups, filling each about 2/3 full.
7. **Bake**:
    - Bake for 20-25 minutes, or until a toothpick inserted into the center of a muffin comes out clean.
8. **Cool**:
    - Let the muffins cool in the tin for a few minutes before transferring them to a wire rack to cool completely.

Tips:

- **Zucchini Moisture**: Squeezing out the moisture from the zucchini is key to preventing overly moist muffins.
- **Add-Ins**: You can add other ingredients like dried fruit, seeds, or even a streusel topping for extra flavor and texture.
- **Storage**: Store the muffins in an airtight container at room temperature for up to 3 days, or freeze for up to 3 months. Reheat in the microwave or toaster oven if desired.

These zucchini bread muffins are a wonderful way to enjoy the benefits of zucchini in a sweet, baked treat. They're moist, flavorful, and perfect for any time of day!

Breakfast Fruit Kabobs

Ingredients:

- 1 cup strawberries, hulled
- 1 cup blueberries
- 1 cup grapes, halved if large
- 1 cup pineapple, cut into bite-sized chunks
- 1 cup kiwi, peeled and sliced
- 1 banana, sliced into rounds
- 1/4 cup honey (optional, for drizzling)
- Fresh mint leaves (optional, for garnish)

Instructions:

1. **Prepare the Fruit**:
   - Wash and cut all the fruit as needed. For the strawberries, remove the green tops. Peel and slice the kiwi. Slice the banana into rounds. If the grapes are large, cut them in half.
2. **Assemble the Kabobs**:
   - Thread the fruit onto wooden or metal skewers, alternating the types of fruit for variety and color. You can create a pattern or simply mix and match. If using wooden skewers, make sure to soak them in water for about 30 minutes before using to prevent burning.
3. **Drizzle with Honey (Optional)**:
   - If desired, drizzle the assembled fruit kabobs with honey for added sweetness. You can also serve the honey on the side for dipping.
4. **Garnish and Serve**:
   - Garnish with fresh mint leaves if desired. Serve the fruit kabobs immediately or refrigerate them until ready to serve.

Tips:

- **Fruit Variety**: Feel free to mix and match fruits based on what's in season or your personal preferences. Other fruits that work well include mangoes, peaches, or melon.
- **Size of Fruit**: Make sure to cut the fruit into pieces that are similar in size to ensure even threading and easy eating.
- **Add-Ons**: For extra flavor, you can sprinkle the fruit kabobs with a bit of cinnamon or a squeeze of lime juice.

Optional Yogurt Dip:

For an added treat, serve the fruit kabobs with a simple yogurt dip:

Yogurt Dip Ingredients:

- **1 cup Greek yogurt** (plain or vanilla)
- **1 tablespoon honey** (or maple syrup)
- **1/2 teaspoon vanilla extract** (optional)
- **1/2 teaspoon lemon zest** (optional)

Instructions:

1. In a small bowl, mix together the Greek yogurt, honey, vanilla extract, and lemon zest until smooth.
2. Serve alongside the fruit kabobs for dipping.

Breakfast fruit kabobs are not only delicious but also visually appealing, making them a great option for entertaining or a healthy breakfast on the go. Enjoy!

Cinnamon Apple Overnight Oats

Ingredients:

- 1 cup old-fashioned rolled oats
- 1 cup milk (any kind—dairy or plant-based like almond, soy, or oat milk)
- 1/2 cup plain Greek yogurt (or regular yogurt, for added creaminess)
- 1 apple, peeled, cored, and diced
- 1 tablespoon chia seeds (optional, for extra fiber and thickness)
- 1 tablespoon honey or maple syrup (adjust to taste)
- 1/2 teaspoon ground cinnamon
- 1/4 teaspoon vanilla extract (optional)
- Pinch of salt

Instructions:

1. **Prepare the Ingredients**:
    - Dice the apple into small, bite-sized pieces. You can use any type of apple, but tart apples like Granny Smith or sweet varieties like Fuji work well.
2. **Mix the Base**:
    - In a medium bowl or a jar with a lid, combine the rolled oats, milk, Greek yogurt, chia seeds (if using), honey, ground cinnamon, vanilla extract (if using), and a pinch of salt.
3. **Add the Apple**:
    - Gently fold in the diced apple, mixing until everything is well combined.
4. **Refrigerate**:
    - Cover the bowl or jar and refrigerate overnight (or for at least 4 hours). The oats will absorb the liquid and flavors, becoming soft and creamy.
5. **Serve**:
    - In the morning, give the oats a good stir. You can add extra toppings like more diced apple, a sprinkle of cinnamon, nuts, seeds, or a drizzle of honey if desired.

Tips:

- **Texture Adjustment**: If you prefer your oats thicker, use less milk. For a creamier texture, add a bit more milk or yogurt.
- **Sweetness**: Adjust the sweetness to your liking. You can add more honey or maple syrup if you prefer it sweeter.
- **Apple Preparation**: For added texture, you can sauté the apples in a bit of cinnamon and a touch of butter before adding them to the oats. This will give them a caramelized flavor.

Optional Toppings:

- **Nuts and Seeds**: Add a handful of walnuts, almonds, or chia seeds for extra crunch and nutrition.
- **Dried Fruit**: Raisins, cranberries, or dried apricots can add a touch of sweetness.
- **Fresh Fruit**: Top with fresh berries, banana slices, or additional apple chunks.

Cinnamon apple overnight oats are a versatile and easy breakfast option that you can customize to your taste. They're perfect for busy mornings and can be a comforting way to start your day!

Egg and Cheese Breakfast Wrap

Ingredients:

- 1 large egg
- 1 tablespoon milk (or cream, optional)
- Salt and pepper, to taste
- 1 tablespoon butter (or oil for cooking)
- 1/4 cup shredded cheese (such as cheddar, mozzarella, or your favorite cheese)
- 1 large flour tortilla (or whole wheat, spinach, or another type of tortilla)
- Optional Add-Ins:
    - 1/4 cup cooked bacon, sausage, or ham (chopped)
    - 1/4 cup diced bell peppers (or other vegetables like onions, spinach, mushrooms)
    - Salsa or hot sauce
    - Fresh herbs (like chives or parsley)

Instructions:

1. **Prepare the Egg Mixture**:
    - In a bowl, whisk together the egg, milk, salt, and pepper until well combined.
2. **Cook the Egg**:
    - Heat a non-stick skillet over medium heat and add the butter or oil. Once melted and hot, pour in the egg mixture.
    - Cook, stirring occasionally, until the egg is fully cooked and scrambled. If using cheese, sprinkle it over the egg just before it finishes cooking so it can melt into the eggs.
3. **Prepare the Tortilla**:
    - While the egg is cooking, warm the tortilla in a separate pan over medium heat for about 30 seconds on each side, or until pliable. You can also microwave it for about 10-15 seconds if preferred.
4. **Assemble the Wrap**:
    - Place the cooked egg mixture in the center of the warm tortilla. If you're adding extra ingredients like bacon or vegetables, sprinkle them over the eggs.
5. **Wrap It Up**:
    - Fold in the sides of the tortilla, then roll it up from the bottom to the top to enclose the filling.
6. **Serve**:
    - Slice the wrap in half if desired, and serve warm. You can also add salsa or hot sauce on the side for extra flavor.

Tips:

- **Make-Ahead**: You can make these wraps ahead of time and refrigerate or freeze them. To reheat, wrap in foil and warm in an oven, or microwave until heated through.

- **Customization**: Feel free to add or substitute ingredients based on your preferences. Try different cheeses, meats, or veggies to create your perfect breakfast wrap.
- **Spicing It Up**: Add spices like paprika, garlic powder, or even a sprinkle of chili flakes to the egg mixture for extra flavor.

Egg and cheese breakfast wraps are a versatile and quick breakfast option that can be tailored to suit your tastes. Enjoy experimenting with different fillings and flavors!

www.ingramcontent.com/pod-product-compliance
Lightning Source LLC
LaVergne TN
LVHW081614060526
838201LV00054B/2254